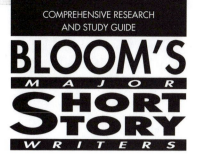

COMPREHENSIVE RESEARCH
AND STUDY GUIDE

BLOOM'S
MAJOR
SHORT STORY
WRITERS

Guy
de Maupassant

EDITED AND WITH AN
INTRODUCTION BY HAROLD BLOOM

CURRENTLY AVAILABLE

BLOOM'S MAJOR
SHORT STORY WRITERS

Sherwood Anderson
Isaac Babel
Jorge Luis Borges
Italo Calvino
Raymond Carver
John Cheever
Anton Chekhov
Joseph Conrad
Julio Cortázar
Stephen Crane
William Faulkner
F. Scott Fitzgerald
Nikolai Gogol
Nathaniel Hawthorne
Ernest Hemingway
O. Henry
Shirley Jackson
Henry James
James Joyce
Franz Kafka
Rudyard Kipling
D.H. Lawrence
Jack London
Thomas Mann
Guy de Maupassant
Herman Melville
Flannery O'Connor
Edgar Allan Poe
Katherine Anne Porter
J.D. Salinger
John Steinbeck
Mark Twain
John Updike
Eudora Welty

COMPREHENSIVE RESEARCH
AND STUDY GUIDE

BLOOM'S
MAJOR
SHORT
STORY
WRITERS

Guy
de Maupassant

CHELSEA HOUSE
PUBLISHERS
A Haights Cross Communications Company

Philadelphia

EDITED AN   LD BLOOM

© 2004 by Chelsea House Publishers, a subsidiary of
Haights Cross Communications.

A Haights Cross Communications ✦ Company

Introduction © 2004 by Harold Bloom.

Printed and bound in the United States of America.

First Printing
1 3 5 7 9 8 6 4 2

Library of Congress Cataloging-in-Publication Data applied for.

ISBN: 0-7910-7587-7

Chelsea House Publishers
1974 Sproul Road, Suite 400
Broomall, PA 19008-0914

www.chelseahouse.com

Contributing Editor: Sarah Robbins

Cover design by Terry Mallon

Layout by EJB Publishing Services

CONTENTS

USER'S GUIDE

This volume is designed to present biographical, critical, and bibliographical information on the author and the author's best-known or most important short stories. Following Harold Bloom's editor's note and introduction is a concise biography of the author that discusses major life events and important literary accomplishments. A critical analysis of each story follows, tracing significant themes, patterns, and motifs in the work. An annotated list of characters supplies brief information on the main characters in each story.

A selection of critical extracts, derived from previously published material, follows each thematic analysis. In most cases, these extracts represent the best analysis available from a number of leading critics. Because these extracts are derived from previously published material, they will include the original notations and references when available. Each extract is cited, and readers are encouraged to use the original publications as they continue their research. A bibliography of the author's writings, a list of additional books and articles on the author and their work, and an index of themes and ideas conclude the volume.

As with any study guide, this volume is designed as a supplement to the works being discussed, and is in no way intended as a replacement for those works. The reader is advised to read the text prior to using this study guide, and to keep it accessible for quick reference.

ABOUT THE EDITOR

Harold Bloom is Sterling Professor of the Humanities at Yale University and Henry W. and Albert A. Berg Professor of English at the New York University Graduate School. He is the author of over 20 books, and the editor of more than 30 anthologies of literary criticism.

Professor Bloom's works include *Shelley's Mythmaking* (1959), *The Visionary Company* (1961), *Blake's Apocalypse* (1963), *Yeats* (1970), *A Map of Misreading* (1975), *Kabbalah and Criticism* (1975), *Agon: Toward a Theory of Revisionism* (1982), *The American Religion* (1992), *The Western Canon* (1994), and *Omens of Millennium: The Gnosis of Angels, Dreams, and Resurrection* (1996). *The Anxiety of Influence* (1973) sets forth Professor Bloom's provocative theory of the literary relationships between the great writers and their predecessors. His most recent books include *Shakespeare: The Invention of the Human*, a 1998 National Book Award finalist, *How to Read and Why* (2000), and *Genius: A Mosaic of One Hundred Exemplary Creative Minds* (2002).

Professor Bloom earned his Ph.D. from Yale University in 1955 and has served on the Yale faculty since then. He is a 1985 MacArthur Foundation Award recipient and served as the Charles Eliot Norton Professor of Poetry at Harvard University in 1987–88. In 1999 he was awarded the prestigious American Academy of Arts and Letters Gold Medal for Criticism. Professor Bloom is the editor of several other Chelsea House series in literary criticism, including BLOOM'S MAJOR SHORT STORY WRITERS, BLOOM'S MAJOR NOVELISTS, BLOOM'S MAJOR DRAMATISTS, BLOOM'S MODERN CRITICAL INTERPRETATIONS, BLOOM'S MODERN CRITICAL VIEWS, and BLOOM'S BIOCRITIQUES.

EDITOR'S NOTE

My Introduction contrasts the benign warmth of "Madame Tellier's Establishment" with the profound horror of "The Horla."

Some of the glories of this volume are Flaubert on "Boule de Suif," John Cowper Powys on "The Necklace," and the formidable trio of Percy Lubbock, Anatole France, and Joseph Conrad on "A Piece of String."

"The Horla" is illuminated by Janko Lavrin. But all twenty-two of the Critical Views are valuable for their insights.

Harold Bloom

Chekhov had learned from Maupassant how to represent banality. Maupassant, who had learned everything, including that, from his master, Flaubert, rarely matches the genius of Chekhov, or Turgenev, as a storyteller. Lev Shestov, a remarkable Russian religious thinker of the earlier twentieth century, expressed this with considerable force:

> Chekhov's wonderful art did not die—his art to kill by a mere touch, a breath, a glance, everything whereby men live and wherein they take their pride. And in the art he was constantly perfecting himself, and he attained to a virtuosity beyond the reach of any of his rivals in European literature. Maupassant often had to strain every effort to overcome his victim. The victim often escaped from Maupassant, though crushed and broken, yet with his life. In Chekhov's hands, nothing escaped death.

That is a very dark view and no reader wants to think of herself as a writer's victim, and yet Shestov accurately weighs Maupassant against Chekhov, rather as one might weigh Christopher Marlowe against Shakespeare. Yet Maupassant is the best of the really "popular" story-writers, vastly superior to O. Henry (who could be quite good) and greatly preferable to the abominable Poe. To be an artist of the popular is itself an extraordinary achievement; we have nothing like it in the United States today.

Checkhov can seem simple, but is always profoundly subtle; many of Maupassant's simplicities are merely what they seem to be, yet they are not shallow. Maupassant had learned from his teacher, Flaubert, that "talent is a prolonged patience" at seeing what others tend not to see. Whether Maupassant can make us see what we could never have seen without him, I very much doubt. That calls for the genius of Shakespeare, or of Chekhov.

There is also the problem that Maupassant, like so many nineteenth- and early-twentieth-century writers of fiction, saw everything through the lens of Arthur Schopenhauer, philosopher of the Will-to-Live. I would just as soon wear Schopenhauerian as Freudian goggles; both enlarge and both distort, almost equally. But I am a literary critic, not a story-writer, and Maupassant would have done better to discard philosophical spectacles when he contemplated the vagaries of the desires of men and women.

At his best, he is marvelously readable, whether in the humorous pathos of "Madame Tellier's Establishment" or in a horror story like "The Horla," both of which I shall consider here. Frank O'Connor insisted that Maupassant's stories were not satisfactory when compared to those of Chekhov and Turgenev, but then few story-writers rival the two Russian masters. O'Conner's real objection was that he thought "the sexual act itself turns into a form of murder" in Maupassant. A reader who has just enjoyed "Madame Tellier's Establishment" would hardly agree. Flaubert, who did not live to write it, wished to set his final novel in a provincial whorehouse, which his son had already done in this robust story.

Everyone in "Mademe Tellier's Establishment" is benign and amiable, which is part of the story's authentic charm. Madame Tellier, a respectable Norman peasant, keeps her establishment as one might run an inn or even a boarding school. Her five sex-workers (as some call them now) are vividly, even lovingly described by Madame's talent for conciliation, and her incessant good humor.

On an evening in May, none of the regular clients are in good humor, because the establishment is festooned with notice: CLOSED FOR A FIRST COMMUNION. Madame and her staff have gone off for this event, the celebrant being Madame's niece (and god-daughter). The First Communion develops into an extraordinary occasion when the prolonged weeping of the whores, moved to remember their own girlhoods, becomes contagious, and the entire congregation is swept by an ecstasy of tears. The priest proclaims that the Holy Christ has descended, and particularly thanks the visitors, Madame Tellier and her staff.

After a boisterous trip back to their establishment, Madame and her ladies return to their ordinary evening labors, performed however with more than the routine zest and in high good spirits. "It isn't every day we have something to celebrate," Madame Tellier concludes the story by remarking, and only a joyless reader declines to celebrate with her. For once, at least, Schopenhauer's disciple has broken loose from gloomy reflections on the close relations between sex and death.

Exuberance in storytelling is hard to resist, and Maupassant never writes with more gusto than in "Madame Tellier's Establishment." This tale of Normandy has warmth, laughter, surprise, and even a kind of spiritual insight. The Pentecostal ecstasy that burns through the congregation is as authentic as the weeping of the whores that ignites it. Maupassant's irony is markedly kinder (though less subtle) than his master Flaubert's. And the story is bawdy, not prurient, in the Shakespearean spirit; it enlarges life, and diminishes no one.

Maupassant's own life ended badly; by his late twenties, he was syphilitic. At thirty-nine, the disease affected his mind, and he spent his final years locked in an asylum, after a suicide attempt. His most upsetting horror story, "The Horla," has a complex and ambiguous relation to his illness and its consequences. The nameless protagonist of the story is perhaps a syphilitic going mad, though nothing that Maupassant narrates actually tells us to make such an inference. A first-person narration, "The Horla" gives us more clues than we can interpret, because we cannot understand the narrator, and do not know whether we can trust his impressions, of which we receive little or no independent verification.

"The Horla" begins with the narrator—a prosperous young Norman gentleman—persuading us of his happiness on a beautiful May morning. He sees a splendid Brazilian three-master boat flow by his house, and salutes it. This gesture evidently summons the Horla, an invisible being that we later learn has been afflicting Brazil with demonic possession and subsequent madness. Horlas are evidently refined cousins of the vampires; they drink milk and water, and drain vitality from sleepers, without actually drawing blood. Whatever has been happening in Brazil, we are free to doubt precisely what is going on in Normandy. Our narrator eventually sets fire to his own house, to destroy his Horla, but neglects to tell the servants, who are consumed with their home. When the tale-teller apprehends that his Horla is still alive, he concludes by telling us that he will have to kill himself.

Clearly it is indeed *his* Horla, whether or not it made the voyage from Brazil to Normandy. The Horla is the narrator's madness, and not just the cause of his madness. Has Maupassant written the story of what it means to be possessed by syphilis? At one point the sufferer glances in the mirror and cannot see his reflection. Then he sees himself in a mist at the back of the mirror. The mist recedes until he sees himself completely, and of the mist of or blocking agent he cries out: "I had seen him!"

The narrator says that the Horla's advent means that the reign of man is over. Magnetism, hypnotism, suggestion, are all aspects of the Horla's will. "He has come," the victim cries out, and suddenly the interloper shouts his name in one's ears: "The Horla ... he has come!" Maupassant invents the name *Horla*; is it an ironic play upon the English word *whore*? That seems very remote, unless indeed Maupassant's venereal disease is the story's hidden center.

The horror story is a large and fascinating genre, in which Maupassant excelled, but never again as powerfully as in "The Horla." I think that it is because, on some level, he knew that he prophesied his own madness and (attempted) suicide. Maupassant is not of the artistic eminence of Turgenev, Chekhov, Henry James, or Hemingway as a short story writer, but his immense popularity is well deserved. Someone who created both "Madame Tellier's Establishment," with its amiable ecstasies, and "The Horla," with its convincing fright, was a permanent master of the story. Why read Maupassant? At his best, he will hold you as few others do. You receive pretty much what his narrative voice gives you. It is not God's plenty, but it pleases many and serves as an introduction to the more difficult pleasures of storytellers subtler than Maupassant.

Guy de Maupassant

Henri René Albert Guy de Maupassant was born on the Normandy coast of France on August 6, 1850, to Gustave de Maupassant, a dandy and an amateur painter with noble roots, and Laure Le Poittevin, a close friend of Gustave Flaubert. Maupassant's mother was determined to pass on her late brother's love of literature and his intellectual awareness to her first son. The family lived in several places around the Normandy area (including Rouen, Fécamp, and Etretat) before settling into the Château de Grainville-Ymauville, near Le Havre. Maupassant's brother Herve was born in 1856, but by 1860, their parents' marriage had dissolved. Gustave Maupassant remained in Paris, while Laure moved her two sons to Etreat, where Guy stayed until in 1863 he became a boarder at the Institution Ecclesiastique in Yvetot.

Since he was rather unhappy at school, Maupassant took refuge in writing. After he was expelled when one of his poems—which compared his soon-to-be-married cousin's happiness with his own misery—was deemed obscene, he enrolled at the Lycée Corneille in Rouen. His guardian there was the writer Louis Bouilhet, a close friend of Flaubert's. Bouilhet's guidance and sense of himself as an artist inspired young Maupassant and rekindled his mother's connection to Flaubert, whose mentorship would eventually shape his career. After passing his baccalaureate in 1869, Maupassant enrolled in a Paris law school and moved into the same apartment block as his father. When France declared war on Germany the next year, he was called up to serve, and after training, he posted as a clerk to Rouen. After the signing of the armistice in early 1871, his father's connections led him to a post at the Ministry's Department for the Colonies.

Enjoying the benefits of a comfortable wage, Maupassant divided his free time between boating and socializing with women in the vacation spot Argenteiul and writing verses, stories, and plays. On Sundays, he visted Flaubert—Maupassant's need for a father figure and teacher after the death of Bouilhet complimented Flaubert's desire for companionship and literary idealism. Flaubert taught Maupassant to be conscientious in his narration, patient in evolving the right means of expression, and discriminating in his choice of words. He also helped his student secure a new job at the Ministry of Education and introduced him to the Parisian literary world of the 1870s, hosting get-togethers with other writers including Ivan Turgenev and Émile Zola.

Flaubert also defended Maupassant when in 1880 he was accused of obscenity for some of his poems. The same year, Zola published an anthology of Naturalist writing called *Les Soirées de Médan*, which included "Boule de Suif," Maupassant's story about the Franco-Prussian war, which he'd likely been working on for several years. Three weeks after hailing the story a masterpiece, Flaubert passed away, inspiring a depression in Maupassant that continued as he traveled to Corsica with his mother. The next year brought the publication of his first short story collection, *La Maison Tellier*, and the continuation of work on a novel he'd started four years earlier, *Une Vie*. During this time, travel and writing occupied his life—the fruits of his labors were compiled in the short-story collection *Mademoiselle Fifi* in 1882, and the publication of *Une Vie* in 1883. The latter has been thought to contain a depiction of Maupassant's parents; it is a good representation of his pessimism and his need to deny some of society's ideals. Despite increasing success Maupassant continued to work tirelessly, until he was immobilized by neuralgia and nearly blind. A consultation with a doctor revealed that these conditions were related to syphilis, with which Maupassant had been diagnosed in1877.

Even illness could not slow Maupassant, however, and as his work earned more acclaim he shared his free time with a high society comprised of writers, artists, journalists, and socialites. He thought his best efforts toward recovering his health and escaping pessimistic thoughts—about human existence, society, and his responsibility as a writer—would be to indulge in luxury. He spent his money on silks, furs, and tropical birds, as well as yachts and homes in places such as Paris and Cannes. Still, despite the distractions, he was prolific—during the 1880s creating about 300 short stories, six novels, three travel books, and one volume of verse. Though the theme of mental disorder was present from the time of *La Maison Tellier*, some of his later works more directly addressed Maupassant's increasing preoccupation with life's purpose and the confounding presence of hallucinations that were a result of his disease. Among these well-regarded tales are the long story "The Horla," a psychological thriller about the presence of invisible forces, and the novel *Pierre et Jean*, a study of two brothers published in 1888, which Henry James would later refer to as a "faultless production."

By the decade's end, Maupassant's ill health had been exacerbated by pressures from work and his brother Herve's descent into madness, subsequent institutionalization, and death. Though Maupassant benefited from advances in medicine, his treatments were so costly he was forced to continue working in order to support himself. In spite of his weakness he completed one more novel, *Notre Cœur*, about the relationship between a rich dilettante and an attractive, high-society hostess. Though he began another, *L'Angelus*, the novel was never finished because his eyes failed and memory blurred. After a visit to his mother on New Year's Day, 1892, he tried to kill himself by slitting his throat with a paper-knife. A few days later he was diagnosed with paresis—the paralysis stage of syphilis—and was committed to a celebrated private asylum in Paris, where he remained until his death on July 6, 1893.

The crowd at Maupassant's funeral was full of the prominent intellectuals and writers he influenced. His legacy continues today—his life representative of the changes France underwent during the second half of the nineteenth century, his work an example of the finest short-story writing. Both emerging and experienced writers imitate his style, and his name is often associated with Tolstoy, Chekhov, Somerset Maugham, and O. Henry.

PLOT SUMMARY OF
"Boule de Suif"

One of Maupassant's first major stories to earn wide audience and acclaim, "Boule de Suif" is based on the true story of a Rouen prostitute—an acquaintance of the author's uncle—who was forced to sleep with a Prussian officer in order to bring food and messages to her lover and his fellow soldiers in Le Havre. When he sent a draft to his mentor, Gustave Flaubert, the author of *Madame Bovary* commended him, saying the story made him laugh out loud a few times.

The story begins in Rouen, where defeated, exhausted-looking soldiers and their leaders have begun to wander in loose bands about the town while shopkeepers flee. Prussians begin entering with measured, organized steps, knocking on citizen's doors and demanding to be quartered. A group of ten people with various commercial interests in Le Havre obtain a permit to leave town. They convene before dawn at the Hôtel de Normandie, and, after much preparation, they set off on their journey in a large, four-horse coach.

Though the carriage rattling through the Normandy countryside contains ten people, eight of them—six members of high society and two nuns—are focused on the other two travelers. One half of this odd couple is Cornudet, a democrat who was recently the victim of a practical joke that led him to think he was appointed prefect of Rouen, and who is hoping to do more good in Le Havre than he had in his hometown. The woman beside him belongs to the courtesan class and is so plump she is nicknamed "Boule de Suif" (Ball of Fat). Cornudet and Boule de Suif's obvious otherness stir within the members of high society feelings of camaraderie—the women united in the sisterhood of legitimized love, the men by the brotherhood of money.

The slow coach is considerably off schedule. By the time one o'clock approaches, Loiseau announces that he has a hollow in his stomach. None of them have thought to bring provisions. At three o'clock Boule de Suif stoops down and extracts a large basket brimming with food and drink. The travelers stare at her, and when Loiseau finally makes a wistful comment, she makes an offer from her basket. Aside from the nuns and Cornudet, who gratefully accept, the rest of the travelers willfully abstain until young Madame Carre-Lamadon faints from hunger and the rest of them concede to partake. Conversation turns toward the war, and then to personal stories. Boule de Suif confesses that though she'd wanted to stay in Rouen, the rage that the Prussian's presence incited in her was too much for her to bear. She says that she flew at one soldier's throat as soon as she got the chance, and that she was forced to hide and then flee after committing such an action. She chides Cornudet, explaining that living in France would be impossible if it were "governed by rascals like you." This exchange inspires appreciation among her fellow travelers; her words, along with her shared food, place her in higher esteem.

Soon the provisions completely disappear and a cold darkness falls, prompting some of the women to lend their foot-warmers to the shivering Boule de Suif. Finally the coach enters Totes and stops at the Hôtel du Commerce. When they enter, they are forced to present their passports to a Prussian soldier. During supper the innkeeper appears and calls out the name of Mademoiselle Elizabeth Rousset. When Boule de Suif responds, the man tells her the Prussian officer wants a word with her. After a bit of protest, Boule de Suif, complies, reminding her fellow travelers that she is doing so for their sakes. Ten minutes later she returns, breathing heavily and calling the man a scoundrel. Though the others inquire about the incident, Boule de Suif is unwilling to share, saying the matter had nothing to do with them.

The innkeeper and his wife join the conversation, and talk turns to war. Cornudet explains that war is a barbaric, but nonetheless sacred duty, and the innkeeper's wife responds with a suggestion to kill all the kings, as they are the ones who make war in the first place. Such a statement prompts Monsieur Carre-Lamadon to think about how the employment of so many idle soldiers would aid great industrial enterprise. Monsieur Loiseau sells several cases of wine to the innkeeper. Soon, when supper is finished and everyone retires to their rooms, Loiseau spies through the keyhole into the hallway; after an hour, he spots Cornudet seemingly suggest to Boule de Suif that she might come back to his room. The young courtesan exclaims her horror, and Cornudet bestows a simple kiss upon her before going back to his room alone.

At eight o'clock the next morning, the travelers assemble in the square with the hopes of setting off. Finally they find the coach driver, who informs them that he has been given orders by the Prussian soldiers not to harness the coach at all. Finally the innkeeper emerges from a late sleep to say the Prussians refuse to let them leave. When the three men ask Cornudet to join them in addressing the Prussian officer at one o'clock, he refuses, saying he wants nothing to do with Germans. The officer denies their request to leave, and before dinner, the innkeeper informs Boule de Suif the soldiers wish to have another word with her.

Angered, she says, "Kindly tell that scoundrel, that cur, that carrion of a Prussian, that I will never consent." When the others bombard her with questions about the nature of these visits, she explains indignantly that the officer wants "me to give myself to him." All appear furious at the news, and save the silent nuns, they offer their sympathy. Everyone retires with the hope of rising early and starting on their way. But the horses and driver are still not ready, and by afternoon, cool feelings toward Boule de Suif are palpable. The count proposes a walk in the village neighborhood, and they set out, leaving behind only Cornudet. Walking ahead of their wives, these men discuss "the trollope" and plot potential means of escape. Suddenly, at the end of the street, the officer appears. The women begin talking about him, and Madame Carre-Lamadon remarks upon his attractiveness, as if to sway the courtesan. The rest of the day is spent in tense silence, and when they come down the next morning, the women barely speak to Boule de Suif. When a pealing church bell indicates a baptism, the courtesan—who has a child at Yvetot that she sees only once a year—leaves to attend the ceremony. In her absence Loiseau suggests they might persuade the officer to detain only Boule de Suif. His wife cites rumors that the courtesan has taken any lover she could get while in Rouen, even coachmen, and contends that the officer had behaved very well. Together the travelers lay their plans to sway her, with each one of them playing a role except for Cornudet. They are so preoccupied with their scheme they don't even notice Boule de Suif's reentry.

When dinner is served the innkeeper asks if Boule de Suif has changed her mind, and she says no. In reference to Boule de Suif's moral dilemma, the countess postulates that several saints have committed acts that might have been seen as immoral in the eyes of the church. The nun eventually says "an action reprehensible in itself often derives merit from the thought which inspires it." The next afternoon the countess proposes a walk, and the count takes the courtesan's arm and tries, with a combination of patient flattery and slight contempt, to convince her to act on their behalf. Though Boule de Suif says nothing, at dinner that night the innkeeper explains her absence by saying the courtesan is not well. When the other travelers realize that she might be with the officer, Loiseau sends around for four bottles of champagne. Yet Cornudet refuses to take part in the revelry, saying, when confronted, that he thinks they have all done an infamous thing. Loiseau then accuses Cornudet of hypocrisy, as he had seen the democrat coerce Boule de Suif himself a few days earlier.

The next morning the coach is finally ready to depart. After some delay, Boule de Suif appears, shamefaced. The count steers his wife away from her, disgusted by potential unclean contact. In turn all of the passengers avoid her, inspiring humiliation and contempt in the woman who has made sacrifices for them. Cornudet says nothing. After three hours, Loiseau announces that he is hungry, and everyone pulls out provisions save Boule de Suif, who has forgotten to do so. At this moment she becomes upset, remembering what of hers they had devoured on the journey to Tôtes, and she begins to weep. Though the travelers slowly notice her despair, they ignore it. Cornudet finishes his food, stretches his legs, smiles, and begins whistling the Marseillaise.

"Boule de Suif"

A member of the courtesan class, Mademoiselle Elizabeth Rousset has earned her nickname **Boule de Suif** because of her short, round body and her face, the shape and shade of a crimson apple. She is nostalgic for a child who she gave up and who now lives in Yvetot. When her traveling party is held up at Totes because she refuses the advances of a Prussian officer who is stationed there, her anxious traveling companions, frustrated by the delay, exploit her naive patriotism by convincing her to sleep with the officer for their mutual benefit. When they finally left Totes, however, the nobles look disdainfully at the courtesan and refuse to share food with her.

A red-bearded, independently wealthy, well-known democrat, **Cornudet's** political views offend the more conservative nobles with whom he travels to Le Havre. Though Monsieur Loiseau catches him propositioning Boule de Suif during their first night in the hotel, later Cornudet refuses to be a part of the plan to persuade Boule de Suif to concede to the Prussian soldier.

After clerking for a failed merchant, **Monsieur Loiseau**, from the Rue Grand-Pont, is now a wholesale wine merchant with a reputation for being a shrewd rascal. His reputation for cheating is so well-established that the citizens of Rouen have come to use the word Loiseau as synonymous with questionable business practice. He spies on an exchange between Boule de Suif and Cornundet during their first night at Totes.

While her husband is the jovial prankster, **Madame Loiseau**, a tall, strong, determined woman, keeps the house in order and the business running.

A proprietor of three cotton mills and a member of the General Council, **Monsieur Carre-Lamadon** is a dignified, cautious man and a member of the highest social caste.

Years younger than her husband, **Madame Carre-Lamadon** is beautiful, slender and graceful. When on principle she refuses to accept an offer of food from Boule de Suif, she grows pale and faint until accepting a few drops of wine.

A neighbor and colleague of the Carre-Lamadons, **Count Hubert de Breville** resembles King Henry IV and has one of the most ancient names in all of Normandy. His income, combined with his wife's, is estimated to be five hundred thousand francs a year.

Rumored to be a former lover of Louis Phillippe's son, the **Countesse Hubert de Breville** has the most exclusive drawing room in the countryside.

Two nuns, one old and permanently scarred from smallpox and the other one, though beautiful, with a sickly countenance, are also bound for Le Havre. They spend most of their stay at Totes at the presbytery. When, in an attempt to persuade Boule de Suif to sleep with the Prussian soldier, the other travelers persuade the nuns to provide God's opinion of the situation, the elder nun's contention that, "An action reprehensible in itself often deserves merit from the thought which inspires it," helps sway the courtesan.

CRITICAL VIEWS ON
"Boule de Suif"

HERBERT ERNEST BATES ON MAUPASSANT'S RELATIONSHIP TO CHEKHOV

[Herbert Ernest Bates was a fiction writer and critic. He is the author of several short-story collections, including the World War II works *The Greatest People in the World*, and *How Sleep the Brave*, and later works such as *The Vanished World* and *The Blossoming World*. Here he examines Maupassant's clarity, ties it to his Naturalist tendencies, and compares and contrasts this technique to Chekhov's often more oblique writing.]

During recent years it has become the fashion to divide both exponents and devotees of the short story into two camps, Maupassant fans on the one side, Tchehovites on the other. On the one side we are asked to contemplate the decisive virtues of the clear, acid, realistic straightforwardness of the French mind, which tells a story with masterly simplicity and naturalism, producing such masterpieces as *Boule de Suif*; on the other hand we are asked to marvel at the workings of a mind which saw life as it were obliquely, unobtrusively, touching it almost by remote control, telling its stories by an apparently aimless arrangement of casual incidents and producing such masterpieces as *The Darling*. (. . .)

As compared with Maupassant, Tchehov will always, I think, seem the slightly more "advanced" and difficult writer. Maupassant, guided by more logical forces, left nothing to chance. Like all writers working within prescribed limits, he was fully aware of the value of a thing implied. By implying something, rather than stating it, a writer saves words, but he also runs the risk that his implication may never get home. That risk, in a very logical French way, Maupassant was less prepared to take than Tchehov. His pictures are more solidly built up; he knows that faces, actions, manners, even the movements of hands and ways of walking are keys to human character; in addition to that he takes a sensuous delight in physical shape, physical response, physical beauty, physical ugliness and behaviour; you can see that nothing delights him so much as a world of flesh and trees, clothes and food, leaves and limbs; in describing such things, as he did so well, he was partially satisfying his own sensuous appetite. That fact gives his every material and physical description a profound flavour. When Maupassant talks of sweat you not only see sweat but you feel it and smell it; when he describes a voluptuous and seductive woman the page itself seems to quiver sensuously. He knew, far better even than Tchehov, which words time and association have most heavily saturated with colour, scent, taste, and strength of emotional suggestion, and it is that knowledge, or instinct, and his skilful use of it, that constitutes one of his most powerful attributes as a writer.

For these reasons Maupassant's appeal will always be more direct and immediate, less subtle and oblique, than Tchehov's. He will always appear to be the greater story-teller, working as he does in the order of physical, emotional, and spiritual appeal. For even if a reader should miss the spiritual touch of a Maupassant story, and even the least subtle of its emotional implications, the physical character of the story would remain to give him a pleasure comparable to that of a woman who has nothing but a physical charm.

This is not of course quite as Maupassant intended. For a Maupassant story is as closely co-ordinated as one of Tchehov; ingredients in it cannot or should not be picked out singly and sampled to the exclusion of others; you cannot pick out the choice morsels of passion and leave the unpleasant lumps of inhumanity, meanness, cruelty, deceit, and falsity which are so important a part of the Maupassant offering. Maupassant too had something to imply as well as something to state. One sees all through his work how money and passion, avarice and jealousy, physical beauty and physical suffering, are dominating influences. Humanity is mad, greedy, licentious, stupid, but beautiful; incredibly base but incredibly exalted. Maupassant, even more than Tchehov, was struck by the terrible irony of human contradictions—contradictions which were so much an integral part of himself that he could not help hating and loving humanity with equal strength. In his attitude to women the force of these contradictions sways him first one way and then another. Women may be prostitutes but they are magnificent, as in *Boule de Suif*; they are rich but they are also depraved; they are poor but generous; they are beautiful but mean; they are divine but deceitful; they may be farm-girls or lonely English virgins, as in *Miss Harriet*, but they are at once pitiable and stupid; they have beautiful bodies but empty heads and, alas, even-emptier hearts.

—Herbert Ernest Bates, *The Modern Short Story: A Critical Survey*, (Boston: The Writer, 1941): pp. 73–74, 91–93.

G. Hainsworth on Flaubert and Schopenhauer

[G. Hainsworth is the author of "Pattern and Symbol in the Work of Maupassant." In this excerpt he explains how Flaubert's exacting simplicity and Schopenhauer's theories on women and the human tendency have influenced both Maupassant's fiction and his journalistic essays.]

We must not forget that Flaubert is handling images, not ideas. Any attempt to bring him in line, from a moral point of view, for example, does violence to his intentions which remain firmly representational and to his vision which inevitably makes of each work, even reduced to its simplest definition (an evocation of perpetual flux in which is included, as its miniature,[100] an impression of human nature and behaviour seized in their general aspect) a monument to *l'éternel néant de tout*.

Flaubert bequeaths to Maupassant, as well as the theory of an impersonal and general art, the theme of illusion-disillusion and human imbecility, with a form which, whether or not presenting that circular pattern to which the subject lends itself, is at all times deliberate.[101] In contrast to the Goncourts, Zola, Daudet, who are interested in the particular, the exceptional, the pathological, almost envisaging the 'document' as an end in itself, and adopt a form which might be defined as that of the broken line and the suspension mark, Flaubert and Maupassant are concerned, over and above any question of mere style, evocation of details, or effects of pathos, with the beauty proper to the work of art, derived from its catholicity and its whole inner arrangement and proportions. It is evident that *Boule de Suif* and *Une Vie*, for example, continue Flaubert in these respects. (…)

Schopenhauer's 'influence' on Maupassant, that is explicit or obvious allusions to Schopenhauer in Maupassant's journalistic essays and elsewhere, has been sufficiently examined by Neubert, Vogl and more recently *Vial*.[103] There is no need here to expand on the references Maupassant makes to the German whenever it is a question of human egoism, sexual relations, the will of the species, women, etc. This is so far true that a difference of opinion may well appear more enlightening than their general agreement. For example, Maupassant considers wives naturally unfaithful, and takes it as a matter of course, whereas Schopenhauer considers fidelity the rule,[104] and deplores adultery on the part of the wife. In general terms, we have to do on one hand with a moralist, a preacher of asceticism, and on the other with one to whom such attitudes are quite foreign. If Schopenhauer explains the infidelity of the husband, the faithfulness of wives and pederasty by reference to the interests of the species,[105] while advocating total abstinence, Maupassant is capable at one moment of recommending voluntary sterility and alembicated modes of intercourse, for a *greater satisfaction* of the senses and as a way of *besting* Nature, and capable at other times of following the *divin marquis* in depicting cruelty and murder as logically falling in with nature's plan. In such a scheme, if one adds that the points listed by Neubert and Vial as illustrating Maupassant's 'pity' would be better classified as notations on the sufferings of the world, not only do morality and renunciation undergo an eclipse, but we enter a labyrinth of scepticism—*l'abîme effrayant du scepticisme* in Pécuchet's phrase[106]—which makes it the more desirable to appeal from what the artist says to what he shows.

100. We may note here Flaubert's remarkable mania for the reduction of opposites, far remote from any *Hegelei*, and tending towards pure negation of reality. We are thinking of the sort of *chassé-croisé* involved when, in *L'Education sentimentale*, Mme Arnoux and Posanette eventually exchange roles, or in *Bouvard et Pécuchet*, the two protagonists (like Don Quixote and Sancho) react on each other and are at times transposed, as also of the basic inspiration of *La Spirale, Une Nuit de Don Juan* and *Harel-Bey*.

101. Cp. our article on Maupassant (*French Studies* V, 1951, pp. 1–17).

103. F. Neubert, *Zeitschrift für Französische Sprache und Literatur, Supplementheft* VIII (1914), pp. 1–78, and IX (1919), pp. 1–130; A. Vogl, ibid., 1938, pp. 83–108; A. Vial, *Guy de Maupassant et l'art du roman*, Paris, 1954. However, if it is a question of *dating* Maupassant's contact with Schopenhauer, *Les Dimanches d'un bourgeois de Paris* and *Héraclius Gloss* would deserve far more attention than they have received.

104. *Metaphysik der Geschlechtsliebe* (vol. II, p. 693); *Parerga* (vol. IV, p. 440).

105. Vol. II, pp. 678–727.

106. *Bouvard et Pécuchet*, p. 283.

107. P. 196.

—G. Hainsworth, "Schopenhauer, Flaubert, Maupassant: Conceptual Thought and Artistic 'Truth.'" *Currents of Thought in French Literature*: (Oxford: Basil Blackwell, 1965): pp. 183–184, 184–185.

MATTHEW MACNAMARA ON MAUPASSANT'S USE OF NATURAL IMAGERY

[Matthew MacNamara is an Associate Professor of French at University College in Cork, Ireland. He is also the author of "Syntax, Clause and Paragraph in the Brouillons of *Madame Bovary*." In this extract, he examines Maupassant's affinity for the *paysage*, or countryside, and how he broadens characterization through natural description.]

The majority of Maupassant's *nouvelles* are texts of no more than a few pages; the length of a small number of longer ones is between thirty and sixty pages of the Forestier edition. When one takes into account the limitations imposed by these restricted dimensions, the place given to description of Nature in the Maupassantian shorter fictional universe is a considerable one. In a genre where the bringing of an anecdote to its dénouement is a fundamental requirement, very many narrators devote a paragraph or two to *paysage*. This descriptive effort is very much in the tradition of Realist fiction particularly as it develops in the novels of the *Rougon-Macquart* series. By a number of its stylistic procedures, notably images of animation and nominal transformations of verbs and adjectives, and by themes of an envelopment of man by the vitality of the natural environment, Maupassant's representations of earth, vegetation, water and light recall some realizations of the Zolian descriptive vision. The Norman orchard enclosed by the grassy banks of its *fossé*, and wooded reaches of the Seine west of Paris are two special *paysages* in the world of Maupassant's *nouvelles*. His narrators' descriptions of each of them are informed by feelings of physical and emotional well-being which are notable in a universe whose themes are so often pessimistic. A description of the pays de Caux farmyard and its environs, seen under strong sunlight, occurs in many stories. (…)

This metaphor of colourful flowers is the basis of a number of other Maupassantian representations of womanhood. In their seductive enterprises his female protagonists blossom. (…)

These analogies and associations make certain colour motifs, and particularly that of redness, privileged forms of the Maupassantian imagination. They give the erotic avidity and destructive conquests of womanhood their place in the vitality of Nature. Associated with blackness redness forms a recurring décor for themes of feminine seduction. In the Maupassantian universe these always involve deception and dissimulation. During erotic approaches the man who imagines his role to be that of hunter is really the unsuspecting prey of a malefic femininity. Red and black are the colours of entrapment and submission of willing male victims. They first appear in a description of *Boule de Suif*'s face with redness shown in a floral image:

Sa figure était une pomme rouge, un bouton de pivoine prêt à fleurir, et là-dedans s'ouvraient, en haut, des yeux noirs magnifiques. (I, 91)   (…)

The Maupassantian vision of femininity sees the distinction between the social roles of wife and courtesan as a superficial one and of the order of appearance. It is underlain by a single womanly nature, that of seductress. Colour motifs re-establish an identity that traditional moral categories, social prejudice and economic hierarchies have blurred. (…)

The Maupassantian renderings of light and liquidity, in Norman, Seine and Mediterranean décors, represent an extraordinarily sensitive contact between a narrative personality and Nature. His descriptions discover in the natural environment an immediate and often aesthetically pleasing material vitality whose beauty acquires from time to time a cosmic perfection. In the Maupassantian shorter fictional world triumphant Nature gives the men who perceive it an experience of total sensual satisfaction. This sensibility, which is primarily a visual one, links his work not only to that of Zola and Flaubert but to that of the Impressionist painters who were his contemporaries. More particularly the place of motifs of interdependent light and liquidity in his imagination gives it an affinity with that of Claude Monet. The recurring narrator whose sensuality brings him so often to abandon himself to the flow of Nature's vitality is the dominant protagonist of the world of Maupassant's *nouvelles*. Much of his fictional existence lies in his creation of *paysages* and the forms which he gives them are rich and personal.

—Matthew MacNamara, *Style and Vision in Maupassant's Nouvelles*, (New York: Peter Lang, 1986): pp. 1–4, 7.

Trevor A. Le V. Harris on Flat and Round Characters

[Trevor A. Le V. Harris is the translator of *Language Through the Looking Glass: Exploring Language and Linguistics*. Here he examines Maupassant's characterization in "Boule de Suif" by evoking E.M. Forster's theory of flat and round characters.]

Where character is concerned, therefore, more so than in other areas, it may be that the antagonism between fiction as play of the signifier, on the one hand, and mimesis, on the other, is no more than a somewhat sterile oscillation between two competing terminologies: whether one is talking about character as a purely verbal construct, as a paradigm of semes which relate it to the events of a given narrative, as a cluster of semantic components with an identifiable 'meaning', as a person-like part of the reality effect or, more simply, as a set of characteristics which evoke a real person, one is ultimately talking about the same thing. It is always a question of seeing characters as more or less complex, more or less rich, more or less deep, as having a greater or lesser number of attributes or traits. In such a perspective, it has to be said that traditional aesthetic or interpretative modes of character appreciation are as valid now as they have ever been, and none more so than the classification proposed by E. M. Forster in his *Aspects of the Novel*. Forster draws a distinction between 'flat' and round' characters:

> Flat characters were called 'humours' in the seventeenth century, and are sometimes called types, and sometimes caricatures. In their purest form, they are constructed around a single idea or quality: when there is more than one factor in them, then we get the beginning of the curve towards the round.

'Round' characters are defined, indirectly, as those characters who are a composition of several or many qualities, characters whom we cannot sum up in any neat formula: 'The test of a round character is whether it is capable of surprising in a convincing way. If it never surprises, it is flat. If it does not convince, it is a flat pretending to be round.'

Flat characters, it might be said, are simple and do not develop in the course of the narrative, while round characters are complex and do develop. The dichotomy is reductive and

Rimmon-Kenan points up the main difficulty with it: 'Although these criteria often co-exist, there are fictional characters which are complex but undeveloping (e.g. Joyce's Bloom) and others which are simple but developing (e.g. the allegorical Everyman).'

Forster's classification none the less provides a useful framework, and the main benefit of the distinction he makes, as a general feature of any author's technique, is that the flatness or the roundness of his characters is an important clue to the author's view of the individual. A greater or lesser insistence on the importance of the inner life of the characters can be taken as the greater or lesser importance for that author of the intrinsic value or accessibility of the individual psyche, as an expression of faith or scepticism regarding the individuality of the human mind one happens to be examining. None of this, of course, is the same as saying that an author's view of his characters is in itself a more or less simplistic technique or that it reveals the degree of intellectual profundity of the author. Because Candide as a character is straightforward, we do not assume that *Candide* is a simplistic piece of literature or that Voltaire is a shallow author. Forster makes the point in relation to Dickensian characters. He underlines their flatness, but adds, 'He is actually one of our big writers, and his immense success with types suggests that there may be more in flatness than the severer critics admit.'

All of which is another way of saying that it is presumptuous of any reader to conflate the simple and the simplistic. With all of these points in mind, one can consider the following brief character description from one of Maupassant's most celebrated stories, 'Boule de suif':

> Cornudet réclama de la bière. Il avait une façon particulière de déboucher la bouteille, de faire mousser le liquide, de le considérer en penchant le verre, qu'il élevait ensuite entre la lampe et son oeil pour bien apprécier la couleur. Quand il buvait, sa grande barbe, qui avait gardé la nuance de son breuvage aimé, semblait tressaillir de tendresse; ses yeux louchaient pour ne point perdre de vue sa chope, et il avait l'air de remplir l'unique fonction pour laquelle il était né. (I, 100)

The success of the description is surely not a function of Cornudet's correspondence, however faithful, to Maupassant's knowledge of a real person on whom the character is based. If this were the case, many readers would fail to appreciate the description. The appeal for the reader lies in Maupassant's skill in manipulating the stereotypical aspects of the portrait. Cornudet is unforgettable because he is so beautifully flat. He is a simple package of a very small number of immediately recognisable qualities. Throughout the story he never surprises us.

Much of the reader's pleasure derives from the comical elements in the description, and this will always remain a wonderful portrait of an old man thoroughly enjoying his glass of beer. And yet, there are a number of points here which, on a closer reading, without detracting from the memorable depiction of Cornudet, begin to undermine the cosy flatness of the character and to create a rather unsettling vision of him as an individual. It is Cornudet's flatness which makes him a memorable character; it is the manner of that flatness which makes him an interesting, yet disturbing character. His beard, for example, has retained the colour of the beer which he consumes almost continuously. The environment has, as it were, left its mark on him. The reduction and repetition of his activity has modified his physical appearance. He is monopolised by that activity. As he drinks he is able to concentrate on nothing else, his beard quivers with pleasure and his eyes cross. The beer consumes Cornudet as much as Cornudet consumes it. There is no nuanced or reasonable reaction to the action. Beyond the comic effect, the implications of this are unsettling. At what one might term a medical level, he is addicted to the beer; it commands his actions. To put the same point in more abstract terms, he is reduced to a state of pure dependency, to something approaching a programmed automaton. The narration draws the reader's attention to this by explicitly stating that Cornudet is performing 'l'unique fonction pour laquelle il était né'.

There *is* a kind of uniqueness about Cornudet. One feels that if one passed him in the street one would recognise him immediately. And yet, that uniqueness proceeds from the photographic accuracy of the description and not from any knowledge we have of Cornudet's personality. We do not need to know people to recognise them from their portrait. In the case of Cornudet, we 'know' him only by a process of inference. Everything is achieved through description of the surface and the assumptions the reader makes about those superficial details. Maupassant, in a sense, seems to invert the old adage and suggests that *l'habit fait le moine.*

—Trevor A. Le V. Harris, *Maupassant in the Hall of Mirrors*, (London: The Macmillan Press Ltd., 1990): pp. 38–41

Gustave Flaubert on "Boule de Suif"

[Gustave Flaubert, 1821–1880, a celebrated French realist and a mentor to Maupassant, is the author of *Madame Bovary*, *A Sentimental Education*, and *The Temptation of Saint-Antoine*, among other novels. In this letter, written a few weeks before his death, he commends his pupil for his hard work and originality.]

"Flaubert's literary disciple as well as a great friend. He was the nephew of Alfred le Poittevin, Flaubert's boyhood friend, which endeared him even more to the other writer. For seven years Maupassant served a severe apprentice ship to Flaubert, and its first result was the famous story *Boule de Suif* proclaimed by Flaubert and subsequently by all the world as a masterpiece." (…)

I have been longing to tell you that I consider *Boule de Suif* a masterpiece. Yes, young man, nothing more nor less than a masterpiece. The idea is quite original, magnificently worked out and excellent in style. The setting and the characters are brought before one's eyes and the psychology is grand. I am delighted with it, in short; and two or three times I laughed aloud.... The little tale will live, I promise you. What a grand bunch your bourgeois are. Not a single failure. Cornudet is immense and lifelike. The nun pitted with smallpox is perfect, and the count

with his 'my dear child', and the ending ... that is grand, too....
Damned if I don't congratulate you again.

—Gustave Flaubert, *Gustave Flaubert: Letters*. Trans. J. M. Cohen,
(London: Weidenfeld and Nicolson, 1950): pp. 231.

Olin H. Moore on Romanticism, Sinful Women, and Lofty Sentiments

[Olin H. Moore is also the author of "How Victor Hugo
Altered the Characters of Don Cesar and Ruy Blas."
Here he discusses Maupassant's relationship to
Romanticism and how it compares and contrasts with his
realist tendencies. Moore illuminates these ideologies by
discussing the writer's interest in the rehabilitated
courtesan in "Boule de Suif."]

In order to arrive at a common understanding of terms, let us
select from the number of classical qualities which, as we have
seen, are frequently credited to Maupassant, two upon which
there is practical unanimity of opinion: (1) his realism, in the
selective sense of the term; (2) his impersonality. It is as a sort of
corollary to these two propositions in particular that critics have
harmoniously advanced the assertion that Maupassant was the
least Romantic of all the realists. We have thus the clue for a
double-barreled definition of Romanticism, which, though
arbitrary, will have at least the advantage of being appropriate to
the occasion. The first term of our definition is suggested by M.
Faguet, according to whose analysis "le fond du romantisme c'est
l'horreur de la réalité et le désir ardent d'y é'chapper. Le
romantisme est essentiellement romanesque."[15] The second
term will be taken from M. Lanson, who, in common with many
other critics, feels that Romanticism is essentially lyrical, or
subjective.[16] Accordingly, all that is realism (in the selective sense
of the term intended by Maupassant himself), all that is
objectivity will be assigned summarily to the category of realism;
all that is "horreur de la réalité," all that is subjectivity, will
similarly assigned to the category of *Romanticism*. (...)

The answer to the question as to what extent Maupassant was Romantic will be found, however, to depend somewhat on general considerations. Shall we limit realism to the narrow meaning understood by the author, as referring only to the immediate present, to the world of sense and flesh? Or shall we understand it in a broader way, as embracing the universe of sense and of flesh, of the past as well as of the present?

I. Let us first meet the author on his own grounds and consider realism only in the narrow meaning which he intended. If we so confine our observations, we shall find that on the whole he gives a greater impression of reality than any other French fiction writer of the nineteenth century. Nevertheless, a close examination will reveal certain Romantic tendencies even here—both in his fundamental point of view and in matters of technique, such as his style and his methods of assembling materials. In his point of view, as we have already begun to note, there was frequently a subjective tendency, an exaggerated *ego*. This excessive emphasis on the *moi* in his writings is proved, (1) by the author's expressed revolt against his mission in life; (2) by the manner in which he carries that spirit of revolt beyond the bounds of his own personality, and puts it into the months of his characters—especially when it is a question of a revolt against law and society in favor of the instincts; (3) by his pleas for emotional justice, the logical result, the logical result of his championship of the instincts against the reason—the author's purpose being, here in particular, clearly propaganda, not an objective study of character; (4) by his occasional revels in the emotionalism of dreams, which he prefers to the harshness of waking reality. (…)

We come now to the consideration of another favorite theme among the writers of the so-called Romantic school—that of the sinful woman ennobled by lofty sentiments in general and by love in particular—by an amorous passion in *Marion Delorme*, and in *la Dame aux camélias*, by maternal affection in *Lucrèce Borgia*. The theme was only a variation of the numerous stories of the outlaw purified by love, as in *Belvédère, Jean Sbogar, Argow le pirate, Bug-Jargal, Hernani*, even in *les Misérables*. The avowed Romanticists who treated this theme might well claim here, as elsewhere, the Middle Ages as their source of inspiration, for had not Guido Guinicelli, in his *Amor e cor gentile*, declared that love, *which purifies all things*, can reside only in a noble heart?

The theme of the rehabilitated courtesan was also treated several times by Maupassant. In *Boule de suif*, the courtesan is the heroine, society is the offender. In the sequel, *Mlle Fifi*,[42] the courtesan is vindicated. After killing a Prussian officer, for patriotic reasons, she was married by a patriot without prejudice, who loved her for her splendid deed, as well as for herself, and "en fit une dame qui valut autant que beaucoup d'autres."

By our definition, was this theme Romantic or realistic?

It appears that it was realistic. We are informed that, so far from being a figment of Romanticism, the heroine of *Boule de suif* and of *Mlle Fifi* actually lived, her real name being Adrienne Legay.[43] In fact, a critic who has made a most valuable contribution to the collection of documents relative to Maupassant assures us that it would have been possible for our author to "inscrire en marge le nom exact de la plupart de ses personnages, avec celui du hameau, du bourg, théâtre de l'action."[44]

Despite such scrupulous *realism*, no basis in fact has yet been offered for the very essential dénoûments of *Boule de suif* and of *Mlle Fifi*. In the case of *Boule de suif*, the only evidence we possess is the indignant denial of the heroine.[45] (...)

Perhaps Maupassant's own enthusiastic declaration that "des filles épousées deviennent en peu de temps de remarquables femmes du monde...."[47] may help to determine whether he had his prejudices in the matter.

NOTES

15. E. Faguet, *Flaubert, cit.*, p. 28.

16. G. Lawson, *op. cit.*, p. 930.

42. A. Lumbroso, *Souvenirs sur Maupassant*, p. 147 and note 1 (*l'Enfance et la jeunesse de Maupassant*, by A. Brisson, being an interview with Mme de Maupassant).

43. A. Lumbroso, *op. cit.*, pp. 351 ff.

44. *Ibid.*, p. 351.

45. *Ibid,*, p. 353.

47. *Réponse à M. Albert Wolff*, in *Mlle Fifi*, p. 279.

—Olin H. Moore, "The Romanticism of Guy de Maupassant." *PMLA* 33, no. 1 (1918): pp. 101, 103–104, 113–114.

"Madame Tellier's Establishment"

The title story of a collection published in 1881, "Madame Tellier's Establishment" is another Maupassant story which comments on societal convention by featuring a prostitute—or in this case a brothel—as the main focus. The brothel girls' exuberant arrival at a country First Communion provides a direct contrast between the sacred and the profane.

Every evening around eleven, six or eight respectable men of Rouen visit Madame Tellier's establishment to drink Chartreuse and laugh and talk with the girls and the proprietor, whom they all greatly respect. The widowed Madame Tellier has taken up her profession as though she might have that of dress making, and she's set up shop inside a house she inherited from an uncle. Tall and stout, the considerate business owner sometimes hires a coach to take her girls into the country for picnics and play.

The house has two entrances and two floors, and two of the regular employees, Louise "La Cocotte" and Flora "The Seesaw," plus Frederic—a short, light-haired, beardless man—wait on the gentlemen in the taproom. The other three women, Fernande, Raphaele, and Rosa, "The Jade," who each represent a different, ideal female type, remain on the first floor to entertain the guests.

One evening near the end of May, former mayor Monsieur Poulin arrives at Madame Tellier's to find the door sealed shut. Confused, he walks to the marketplace and finds several other bourgeois customers bound for the place. Together they return to the house to make another attempt at entry. As they are already incredibly irritated, a quarrel breaks out among some of them, and as the defeated disperse, a few others witness a fight break out among English and French soldiers. Finally the last man standing, the fish-curer, Monsieur Tournevau, examines Madame Tellier's walls for an explanation. He is surprised to find a sign posted to a shutter which reads CLOSED FOR FIRST COMMUNION.

Madame Tellier's brother, Joseph Rivet, a carpenter who lived in their hometown of Virvillle, has a 12-year-old daughter, Constance, who is about to make her First Communion. He wants his sister present in part because her good financial standing might benefit his daughter. Rivet is not troubled by Madame Tellier's occupation; the other residents of the town, none of whom had ever strayed farther than Rouen, know anything about it. Since Madame Tellier is certain she cannot leave business operating as usual, as fights might break out among the staff, she resolves to bring all of them along, save Frederic, whom she gives a holiday.

Dressed in their finest, the women board a second-class carriage that Saturday. When they arrive at Bolbec, a man carrying parcels boards the train and they steer the conversation towards what they imagine might impress others. The girls scramble all over the man to coo over the basket of ducklings he's brought on board. Then he pulls a parcel out and, making a joking comment about suspenders, presents a wide array of garters with the offer of a pair to anyone willing to try them on. After some coercion, all of the women, including Madame Tellier, accept a pair.

When they arrive, Rivet meets them at the station with a large, horse-drawn cart. On the way back to his home, the women take in the beautiful, green countryside, exclaiming over the blue cornflowers and red poppies. After a midday meal with Madame Rivet, they go for a stroll. As they walk, the children stop playing, the townspeople halt their everyday activities and peek through their curtains, and a few old women even cross themselves upon witnessing the parade of resplendent city people. When they pass the church and hear young people singing, Madame Tellier refuses to let the girls enter, lest they disturb the children's practice. After supper they make ready for bed and sleep two-by-two, save Rosa, who sleeps alone in a little cupboard. Unable to sleep, Rosa hears the faint cries of Constance, who, having been ordered to sleep in the attic instead of with her mother, is afraid. She fetches the child, who falls fast asleep with her head on the courtesan's bosom. At five o'clock the next morning the church bells ring and awaken the women, who are used to sleeping the morning away. After dressing they walk in a large procession through the village to the church. When they enter, the congregation grows excited by the sight of such elaborate dresses and the mayor offers them his pew.

Toward the end of the service, Rosa's thoughts turn to her mother, her church, and her own First Communion, and she begins to cry. Tears also fall on the faces of Louise and Flora, who have similar recollections, and soon Madame Tellier finds that her own eyes are wet. Around the congregation, mothers, daughters, and finally men bow their heads and sob. The effect is like a gust of wind blowing through the church. Finally the priest raises his hand to command silence, makes a few remarks about what has just happened, and attributes the phenomenon to a miracle. He thanks Madame Tellier and her girls, whose "evident faith and ardent piety have set such a salutary example to all." After the service they surround the little girl and kiss her, Rosa being the most demonstrative of all. The following dinner is subdued, although Rivet is drinking to excess. He tries to distract his sister as to keep the guests until the next day, but Madame Tellier will have none of it. Rivet's wife tries to engage her sister-in-law in a conversation about the future of the girl, but nothing is settled.

Meanwhile Rivet, in his stupor, begins flirting with Rosa. Given the tenor of the morning's ceremony, some of the women are surprised by his actions, though others encourage him. Madame Tellier seizes her brother by the shoulders and throws him out of the room; a few moments later he reappears with the horse and cart. On their way Fernande asks Rosa to sing, and after a quashed attempt at "Gros Cure de Meudon"—a song Madame Tellier deems inappropriate—they all join in to sing "The Grandmother." In response to Rivet's regrets that the women cannot stay longer, Madame Tellier informs him that the women cannot always be enjoying themselves. Rivet, eying Rosa, promises to pay a visit to Fecamp later in the month, and, hearing the train whistle, kisses all of them, trying for Rosa's mouth.

The women return to the house refreshed, and Madame Tellier exclaims that she has had a good time, though she was anxious to get home. They eat their supper quickly and make ready for their customers, hanging a lantern outside to indicate they are open for business. The banker's son, upon hearing the news, interrupts Monsieur Tournveau's Sunday dinner to inform him the women have returned. Soon the house, which has a festive holiday look, is filled with regular customers and rocking with dancing and flirting. Most of the drinks are free, because as Madame Tellier says, "We don't have a holiday every day."

"Madame Tellier's Establishment"

When **Madame Tellier** inherited a house from her uncle, she and her husband, formerly innkeepers at Yvetot, set up an "establishment" in Fechamp where men would come, drink, and socialize with the ladies. After her husband's death, Madame Tellier continues to employs "her girls" in the thriving brothel where she is well-respected by both clients and employees for her refined mind. When her niece is confirmed in Virille, she is compelled to bring her family of girls along.

A handsome blonde and the ideal "country girl" hand-selected by Madame Tellier, **Fernande** is tall, fat, and lazy.

A native of Marseilles, **Raphaele** is the ideal, handsome Jewess. Her beauty—high cheekbones and black hair—is spoiled neither by a speck in her right eye or her two false upper teeth.

A tireless talker and lover of food, **Rosa** "the Jade" is a little roll of fat whose laugh resounds throughout Madame Tellier's establishment. The night she stays with the Rivets, she hears the cries of Constance, their daughter, and she fetches the child to come sleep with her. In the morning, at Constance's First Communion, thoughts of her own family provoke a flood of tears in Rosa, which in turn sets off the entire congregation.

Louise and **Flora**, who work on Madame Tellier's ground-floor and physically resemble servants at an inn, are often referred to as the "two pumps." Though they don't play a very prominent role in the festivities, they also accompany the other three girls and Madame Tellier to the First Communion.

A carpenter in the Department of Eure, **Joseph Rivet** invites his sister to come witness the First Communion of his daughter Constance in part so Madame Tellier might have a chance to offer financial support to the girl as she comes of age. Caught up in the celebration, he makes several passes at Rosa. Though he offers to have his sister and the girls to spend another night with his family, the invitation is declined.

A devoted wife and mother, **Madame Rivet** makes a big scene of welcoming her sister-in-law and the guests to their home for Constance's First Communion. Right before Madame Tellier's departure, Madame Rivet makes a point of cornering her in an attempt to discuss the child's future.

Among the devoted customers of Madame Tellier's, **Monsieur Tourneveau**, the fish-curer; **Monsieur Poulin**, the former-mayor; **Monsieur Phillippe**, the banker's son; and **Monsieur Dupis**, the insurance agent, are especially disturbed to find a sign posted that read mysteriously "Closed for First Communion." Monsieur Phillippe is so delighted to learn of the establishment's reopening that he even sends a cryptic telegram to Monsieur Tournevau.

CRITICAL VIEWS ON
"Madame Tellier's Establishment"

MARTIN TURNELL ON THE BROTHEL

[Martin Turnell was a critic and frequent contributor to
the New York Review of Books. He is the author of *Jean
Racine, Dramatist* and *The Novel in France*. In this excerpt
he discusses Maupassant's juxtaposition of the House of
God with the House of Love.]

The brothel possessed an extraordinary fascination for
nineteenth-century French writers. It was an obvious stick to
beat the bourgeois, an easy way of exposing their hypocrisy and
scoring off the 'old goats' who escaped from their pious, long-
faced wives for an evening's fun among the gilt and the plush. It
also had a deeper significance. It was a reflection of the
fundamental nihilism of the age. The writers imagined that they
had got rid of religion. The next step was to get rid of man, to
reduce him to a bundle of instincts, to turn love into a
commodity which was bought and sold, into the tangle of hairy
legs and frilly bloomers among the rumpled sheets that we find
in one of Maupassant's bolder illustrators.

In *La Maison Tellier*, as in other stories, Maupassant adapts the
conte leste to his particular purposes. It is an account of a school
treat transposed into a somewhat unexpected setting. The visit of
Madame and her staff to her brother's, for the First Communion
of her niece, fulfils the same object as the expedition in *Boule de
Suif*. It enables him to study a corner of society at close quarters.
It also provides ample scope for his comedy: the encounter with
the commercial traveller in the train, the villagers rushing to
their doors to gape at the 'belles dames', the old lady crossing
herself as the grotesque troop goes by in the belief that it is a
religious procession, the visitors 'gushing' over the first
communicant and helping to dress her, the 'régiment Tellier'
setting out for the ceremony with Madame at its head, the
hysteria in church, the father 'getting, fresh' with the girls and
being sternly rebuked by his sister.

The story is built round the familiar contrasts: the House of God and the House of Love, the *curé* and Madame with their respective flocks which are significantly united in the moment of hysteria, the fragrant open countryside and the hot, fetid, noisy brothel. The theme of prostitution-patriotism re-emerges as respectability-prostitution. From the outset, Maupassant goes to considerable lengths to establish the 'respectability' of Madame and the decorousness of her establishment. This is the opening paragraph which consists of a single sentence:

> On allait là, chaque soir, vers onze heures, comme au café, simplement.

> [You went there, every evening, about eleven, as though it were a café, simply.]

The punctuation and the trailing Flaubertian adverb give the impression of the clients sauntering in, as though it were the most innocent and the most natural thing in the world. It goes on:

> Ils s'y trouvaient à six ou huit, toujours les mêmes, non pas des noceurs, mais des hommes honorables, des commerçants, des jeunes gens de la ville; et l'on prenait sa chartreuse en lutinant quelques peu les filles, ou bien on causait sérieusement avec *Madame*, que tout le monde respectait.

> [There were six or eight of them there, always the same ones, not rakes, but upright men, tradespeople, young men from the town, and you drank your Chartreuse and teased the girls a bit, or you conversed seriously with Madame, whom everybody respected.]

In spite of her profession Madame is, in her way, a model of virtue who is shocked by an improper word or an indecent story. The clients who had hoped for her favours after the death of her husband have been disappointed. Although Maupassant's aim is clearly to make her into an adequate foil for the *curé*, to link respectability and religion, his real interest is in the denouement. On the last page she makes an assignation with the local judge. It is another equation. The foolish *curé* mistakes hysteria for a miracle; respectability and prostitution cancel out; the answer is another zero.

The sentence which records the fall of Madame deserves notice:

> M. Vase, who in the past had danced on social occasions, did the honours and Madame gave him a captivated look, that look which says 'Yes' more discreetly and more delightfully than any spoken word.

Its blatant vulgarity is typical of many other sentences in the story such as the comparisons between the brothel and the sanctuary lamps, or the account of the first communicant spending the night with her head reposing on the bosom of one of the prostitutes. *La Maison Tellier* is written with Maupassant's customary dexterity, but the theme was a temptation rather than an opportunity. Far from being one of his most notable achievements, the story exhibits all his characteristic, vices—his crudity, his facile cynicism, a fundamental lack of intelligence.

—Martin Turnell, *The Art of French Fiction*, (London: Hamish Hamilton; New York: New Directions, 1959): pp. 206–208.

PROSSER HALL FRYE ON MAUPASSANT'S EYE FOR DETAIL

[Prosser Hall Frye is the author of *Romance and Tragedy: A Study of Classic and Romantic Elements in the Great Tragedies of European Literature*. In this excerpt he argues that "Madame Tellier's Establishment" is the best example of Maupassant's precise depiction of sensation, which in turn allows the story to live up to its writer's contention that it is "short, unique, and as perfect as it can possibly be made."]

One becomes only the more convinced, the more one studies him, that style was his sole concern, and that his illusion was only a reflection of life, as adventitious and arbitrary as the original itself. Even his cynicism is the inadvertent cynicism of accident, and depends largely on the incongruity of circumstances. If there seems at first sight to be a significance of choice in his themes, as though he believed the world in truth to be as sordid as he represents, and picked his subjects accordingly, this apparent significance resolves on consideration into an instinctive preference for the kind of thing that he could do best. Nor is it possible, on the other hand, to overlook from page to page traces of a deliberate effort to obliterate what vestiges of intelligent design have slipped into his creation, and to give his mimic world an air of wanton and irresponsible fortuity. (…)

His senses were extraordinarily keen; and his writing is spangled with numerous little images of almost crystalline hardness and brilliancy, like particles of quartz and mica in a gravel path. Anything that offered an edge or a surface, the ordures of Paris or the paunch of a *bourgeois*, a stigma or a deformity, he was certain of catching with a vividness hardly less than marvellous. For this reason his figures, though they stand for little or nothing, have a solidity, a plasticity, which is not Greek, though there is nothing else to compare it with. In fact, so far does he carry this method of portraiture that it is a fair question whether he was not capable of gratuitous distortion, as he was of partial selection, for the sake of enhancing the poignancy of his expression. A writer's real theory usually consists in the discovery of the kind of thing that he can do best; and it was, as a matter of practice, in the superficial adjustment between expression and the sharp somatic thrill of things, the smart and tingle of sensation, that he set his ambition, without other care than just this rather unintelligent one, for the significance of his subject. To this effect he quotes Flaubert with ingenuous approval:

> "When you pass," he [Flaubert] used to say, "a grocer sitting at the door of his shop, a janitor smoking his pipe, a stand of hackney coaches, show me that grocer and that janitor, their attitudes, their whole physical appearance,

embracing, likewise, as indicated by the skilfulness of the picture, their whole moral nature, so that I cannot confound them with any other grocer or any other janitor. Make me see, in one word, that a certain cab horse does not resemble the fifty others that follow or precede it."

This was his ideal—the thing he actually tried to do; and *La Maison Tellier*, from which I recently quoted, is probably his most successful realisation of it. "I perceived," he observes toward the close of his essay on the novel—and the contrast with Zola's notion of "big machines" is remarkable—"that the best writers have very seldom left more than one volume; and that before all things it is necessary to have the opportunity of finding, amid the multiplicity of matters presented to our choice, that which will absorb all our faculties, all our work, and all our artistic powers." *La Maison Tellier* fortunately fills no volume, but it is the result of some such favourable coincidence as this. The subject, which is as usual quite unspeakable, seems to have been singularly well adapted to his temperament and his technique, and the story is, therefore, thoroughly representative of his peculiar powers—a work hard, senseless, and irrelevant, but, according to his own definition, "short, unique, and as perfect as it can possibly be made."

—Prosser Hall Frye, *Literary Reviews and Criticisms*, (New York: Gordian Press, 1908): pp. 197–198, 200–202.

MARY DONALDSON-EVANS ON AMBIGUOUS RELIGIOUS CONVICTION

[Mary Donaldson-Evans, a Professor of language and literature at the University of Delaware, has been a recipient of a fellowship from the National Endowment for the Humanities. She is the co-editor of *Modernity and Revolution in Late 19th-Century France*. She discusses here how Maupassant handled the prevalent disaffection for religion during his era and how he channeled some of this moral ambiguousness into his depiction of prostitutes' trip to church.]

The disaffection for traditional religion that was prevalent at the end of the 19th century in France had many sources, literary, philosophical, scientific, historical. France's sobering defeat at the hands of the Prussians in the War of 1870 shattered French self-confidence; the horrors of the Commune even further shocked the nation and plunged her into an emotional depression from which she did not fully emerge until the end of the century. Marked by a resurgent interest in Romanticism's dark side, the literature of this period reflects the pessimism of the day, a faithless pessimism that found the roots of its disbelief in the determinism of Darwin and Taine, the cynicism of Schopenhauer and the tradition of blasphemy going back to Sade.

A superficial reading of Maupassant's work suggests that he was in perfect step with the *fin-de-siècle* skepticism preached by his contemporaries. The profanatory spirit in which he makes use of religious themes and décors conforms precisely to what Jean Pierrot terms "le catholicisme esthètique" (*L'Imaginaire décadent*, 106) of the decade beginning in 1880, that is, the use by non-believing writers of religious subjects solely for artistic effect, for the *pittoresque*. And yet a closer analysis of Maupassant's treatment of religious themes reveals unsuspected complexities, as well as a contempt for the concept of God which cannot be traced uniquely to the "hors-texte" of his era, but which is closely bound to the role played by women in his fictional universe. (…)

This absence of scruples in even the most "religious" of Maupassant's heroines is everywhere apparent. Cogny has pointed out that, according to a common prejudice of the period, "un homme qui pratique est un sot, et une femme qui ne pratique pas une gourgandine" (*Maupassant*, 41). The corollary of this statement—the woman who does practice her religion is virtuous—does not apply to the world contained in Maupassant's fiction, where harlots are endowed with a religious fervor far exceeding that of most women, and for good reason. If the

Goncourts had bequeathed to Maupassant the notion that religion satisfied a woman's sexual needs, or, put somewhat less crudely, that woman's sexuality and her religiosity had a common source ("La religion est une partie du sexe de la femme," they had proclaimed in an 1857 entry to their *Journal*), Maupassant was quick to draw the obvious conclusion: the more "sexual" the woman, the greater her capacity for religious ecstasy. One has only to consider Boule de Suif, who derives immense satisfaction from prayer, or the prostitutes of "La Maison Tellier," whose uncontrollable weeping during a First Communion service gains an entire congregation and causes the priest to assert with considerable emotion that a miracle has taken place in his church:

> Pendant que Jésus-Christ pénétrait pour la première fois dans le corps de ces petits, le Saint-Esprit, l'oiseau céleste, le souffle de Dieu, s'est abattu sur vous, s'est emparé de vous, vous a saisis, courbés comme des roseaux sous la brise. (I, 275)

It must have been with mirthful malice that Maupassant selected his priest's words, whose *double-entendre* brings to mind monstrous visions of Christ as rapist, the Holy Spirit as vulture and man not as *roseau pensant*, to use Pascal's image, but rather as a fragile reed battered by emotion in the "wind" of God's breath. The mockery that can be discerned at the lexical level is consistent with the symbolism of the narrative itself: the emotional frenzy into which the congregation has been thrown is not divinely, but humanly inspired, and the source of the inspiration is a prostitute whose reminiscences of childhood purity move her to tears. Inasmuch as their profession demands that they raise their customers to an orgasmic pitch of passion, in the communion scene the prostitutes have merely transferred from the physical to the emotional plane their role as *allumeuses*, and the renewed enthusiasm with which they undertake their normal duties later the same day appears not as alien, but as complementary to the contagious excitement they had felt in the church, *maison de Dieu* which is an obvious counterpart of the *maison de passe* in which the women work. To the communion wine thus corresponds the champagne offered gratis to all customers that evening. "Ça n'est pas tous les jours fête," explains the radiant madam in the story's closing line.

—Mary Donaldson-Evans, *A Woman's Revenge: The Chronology of Dispossession in Maupassant's Fiction*, (Lexington, KY: French Forum Publishers, 1986): pp. 82, 83–84.

CHARLES J. STIVALE ON THE RELATIONSHIP BETWEEN WOMEN AND THEIR CLIENTELE

[Charles J. Stivale is a Professor of French at Wayne State University. He is the author of *Two-Fold Thought of Deleuze and Guattari* and *Disenchanting Les Bons Temps*. In this extract he discusses the relationship between the ladies of Madame Tellier's establishment and their bourgeois clientele, and the contrast between events holy and carnal.]

In "La Maison Tellier," the sole tale by Maupassant that focuses its primary attention on the brothel inhabitants and on their bourgeois clientele, the rupture between the characters is not explicitly internal, as in "Boule de suif." Rather, the strategy consists of constructing the appearance of nearly blissful harmony while deploying the textual war-machine, in fact, against *l'homme-fille* through his relations with the *filles*. This strategy suggests a dual consideration of the tale: I will observe, on one hand, the function of the seemingly mystical transformation that the *filles* and the proprietress of the *maison*, Madame Tellier, undergo during their trip to attend a first communion in the latter's home village. On the other hand, I will scrutinize the role played by the bourgeois clientele in terms of the transformation of their relations with the occupants of the *maison*. By following the key moments of this transformation in the tale's three sections—the preparation for change implicitly announced with the *maison*'s unexpected closure on a Saturday night in rural Fécamp, the transformative trip on Saturday and

Sunday, and the metamorphosis of activities in the re-opened *maison* on Sunday evening—I will study how Maupassant deploys the art of rupture as a weapon aimed at *filles* as well as at *hommes-filles*.

From the first sentence onward—"Men went there every evening about eleven o'clock, just as they went to the café" (CSS 43) [On allait là, chaque soir, vets onze heures, comme au café, simplement (CN 1:256)]—,the tale suggests that its focus and frame consist precisely of the relationship of the *filles* to *hommes-filles*, of the *maison* to its clientele, between which occur the women's excursion and transformation. The nominative devices employed to designate the distinction of the proprietress are, first, the author initially placing her title, *Madame*, in italics and, second, the narrator noting emphatically that "Madame, who came of a respectable family of peasant proprietors in the department of the Eure, had taken up her profession, just as she would have become a milliner or dressmaker," for a simple reason:

> The prejudice against prostitution, which is so violent and deeply rooted in large towns, does not exist in the country places in Normandy. The peasant simply says: "It's a paying business," and sends his daughter to keep a harem of fast girls, just as he would send her to keep a girls' school. (CSS 43; CN 1:256)

That this observation is an extraordinary example of wish-fulfillment alerts us to the perspective of *l'homme-fille* preparing the tale's dénouement: whereas Madame Tellier's operation of the *maison* and management of the *filles* correspond to laudable business practices, this submission to bourgeois principles will nonetheless yield finally, during one golden evening at least, to the generative, seductive principle of the art of rupture. For not only does the reader observe the wise distribution of female resources in the *maison*, specifically, two *filles* (Louise, "nicknamed Cocote," and Flora, "called Balançoire [the swing] because she limped a little") for the commoners in the downstairs café, and three *filles* (Fernande, *la juive* Raphaële, and "a little roll of fat," Rosa la Rosse) (CSS 45; CN 1:258–59) for the bourgeois clients upstairs in the salon. The reader also learns an important detail of the widow Tellier's character: that, besides exhibiting exemplary refinement, reserve, and maternal solicitude, "since Madame had been a widow, all the frequenters of the establishment had wanted her, but people said that personally she was quite virtuous" (CSS 44) [absolument sage (CN 1:257)]. To her clients, her presence above the demands of her calling served the vital and shrewd marketing function of providing "a rest from the doubtful jokes of those stout individuals who every evening indulged in the commonplace amusement of drinking a glass of liquor in company with girls of easy virtue" (CSS 44; CN 1:258).

Given that her *maison* had become for her bourgeois clientele "a resource" and that they "very rarely missed their daily meetings there" (CSS 45; CN 1:260), it is understandable that their finding the *maison* inexplicably closed one Saturday evening would throw the group into disarray. The depiction of their plight is quite instructive since Maupassant does not fail to attach each name to a civil status. Thus, M. Duvert ("the gunmaker"), M. Poulin ("timber merchant and former mayor"), M. Tournevau ("the fish curer"), M. Philippe ("the banker's son"), M. Pimpesse ("the collector"), M. Dupuis ("the insurance agent"), and M. Vasse ("the judge of the tribunal of commerce") all find the doors shut. M. Tournevau is especially "vexed" since "he, a married man and father of a family and closely watched, only went there on Saturdays—*securitatis causa*, as he said, alluding to a measure of sanitary policy which his friend Dr. Borde had advised him to observe. That was his regular evening, and now he would be deprived of it for the whole week" (CSS 46; CN 1:260). joining four other regulars, the "sad promenaders" wander listlessly, M. Poulin ("timber merchant and former mayor") and M. Dupuis ("insurance agent") nearly coming to blows in their frustration, and a group of four eventually returns "instinctively" to the still "silent, impenetrable" *maison*. Much later, wandering alone, "exasperated at the police for thus allowing an establishment of such public utility, which they had under their control, to be thus closed," M. Tournevau discovers the notice that had been posted on a shutter all along, "Closed on account of first communion" (CSS 47; CN 1:262), a statement that "emphasizes the equation *maison–commercial establishment*" and partially clarifies the enigma of the *maison*'s closure that dominates the opening sequence (Dickson 45–46).

Madame Tellier's purpose for taking the five *filles* in her employ along to the country birthplace, in fact, follows sound business practice since the canny proprietress wants to avoid the consequences of difficulties that would inevitably arise in her absence: the "rivalries between the girls upstairs and those downstairs," the drunkenness of the footman, Frédéric, events that would upset the smooth functioning of her establishment. The majestic effect of these women on the quiet village— whether on a simple promenade that becomes "a procession" before the villagers (CSS 51; CN 1:268), on their way to the church as "Madame Tellier's regiment" (CSS 53; CN 1:271), or at the mass and communion ceremony in the tiny church—is indeed impressive, all the more so since their profession is unknown in this isolated rural community. But of greater importance for the implicit development of the narrative war-machine is the effect of this environment itself on these women that contributes to producing a profound metamorphosis. This process is initiated as much by the attitude of Madame's niece, "the well-behaved child, fully penetrated by piety, as if closed off through absolution" (CN 1:269) [l'enfant bien sage, toute pénétrée de piété, comme fermée par l'absolution (omitted from translation)], as by the "perfect repose of the sleeping village," causing the visitors to shiver, "not with cold, but with those little shivers of solitude which come over uneasy and troubled hearts" (CSS 51; CN 1:269). That night in the village is particularly difficult for one *fille*, Rosa the Jade (Rosa la Rosse), "unused to sleeping with her arms empty" (CN 1:269), until she goes to comfort Madame Tellier's sobbing and frightened niece, taking her back into her bed where Rosa "lavished exaggerated manifestations of tenderness on her and at last grew calmer herself and went to sleep. And till the morning the girl slept with her head on Rosa's naked bosom" (CSS 52) [Et jusqu'au jour la communiante reposa son front sur le sein nu de la prostituée (CN 1:270)].

This astonishing juxtaposition of the sacred and the profane and, following Michel Crouzet, the "permanent conflict between farce and its conjuration" (248), establish an implicit destabilization of bourgeois commonplace images, a fact not lost on the (anonymous) English translator who systematically distorts the original by rendering *communion* by *confirmation*, *communion recipient* by *confirmation candidate*, and extensively censoring the consecration scene that follows. During the mass, Rosa is again at the center, this time of the veritable outbreak of "contagious weeping." For having recalled her own first communion, her sobbing transmits throughout the church a "strange sympathy of poignant emotions" that affects everyone: "Men, women, old men and lads in new blouses were soon sobbing; something superhuman seemed to be hovering over their heads—a spirit, the powerful breath of an invisible and all-powerful being" (CSS 54; CN 1:274). Receiving communion from the "old priest," the people "opened their mouths with spasms, nervous grimaces, eyes closed, faces pale" (CN 1:274; omitted from translation). Then,

> Suddenly a species of madness seemed to pervade the church, the noise of a crowd in a state of frenzy, a tempest of sobs and of stifled cries. It passed over the people like gusts of wind which bow the trees in a forest, and the priest remained standing, immobile, the host in his hand, paralyzed by emotion, saying: "It's God, it's God who is among us, who is manifesting his presence, who is descending as I speak to his kneeling congregation." And he stammered out incoherent prayers, those inarticulate prayers of the soul, in a furious burst toward heaven. (CSS 54; CN 1:274)

His no doubt heartfelt final words are turned cruelly ironic from the perspective of the textual war-machine, for in seeking to calm the crowd, the priest bestows a special benediction on the visitors "whose presence among us, whose evident faith and ardent piety have set such a salutary example to all." "Without you," he continues, "this day would not, perhaps, have had this really divine character. It is sufficient at times that there should be one chosen to keep in the flock, to make the whole flock blessed" (CSS 54) [Il suffit parfois d'une seule brebis d'élite pour décider le Seigneur à descendre sur le troupeau (CN 1:274)]. Finally, "his voice failed him again from emotion, and he added, 'I wish for you divine grace. So be it'" [C'est la grâce que je vous souhaite. Ainsi soit-il (CN 1:275; omitted from translation)]. (...)

However, as if to explain not only this truly inconceivable generosity, but also the general willingness that contributes to maintaining the euphoric atmosphere, Madame, "who was beaming, said to them: 'It's not every day that we have a holiday'" [Ça n'est pas tous les jours fête]. Yet, as has been amply noted (Crouzet 248–49; Dickson 49–50), this final statement contains not merely the focal ambiguity between the determining festive events, holy (first communion) and carnal (the homecoming). It also underscores the ambiguity of Madame's intentions: on one hand, she may provide a recapitulative "justification" of these activities, drawing into her radiant joy readers and customers alike. On the other hand, this justification may also serve as a prospective, business-like limitation to such generosity, to the *fête* that does and will not come everyday, when business as usual will certainly prevail. The latter reading is supported by the fact that, unlike the euphoric abandon of the women under her charge, Madame negotiates at length with M. Vasse before yielding anything from her precious "capital" amassed over the years—her reputation as being "absolument sage," not only virtuous, but wise. This reading situates the tale finally within the letter of the Law, albeit one that an empowered woman (relatively so, of course, within an oppressive patriarchal framework) chooses to exercise according to her principles of exchange and usage, but within an "establishment of public utility" (CSS 47; CN 1:262) that must respect its commercial function and thereby maintain the proper balance between conjugal and sensual pursuits.

—Charles J. Stivale, *The Art of Rupture: Narrative Desire and Duplicity in the Tales of Guy de Maupassant*, (Ann Arbor: University of Michigan Press, 1994): 114–118, 119.

"The Necklace"

One of a series of short, realistic tales centered on the premise of a single object, "The Necklace" is a strikingly accurate depiction of a relationship between husband and wife. With an ironic surprise ending, the story illustrates how a strong sense of pride can both create opportunity and disaster in a marriage.

Mathilde is a charming girl who covets luxury, but since she has been born to a family of clerks and has no dowry, she is forced to make do marrying Monsieur Loisel, a clerk in the Ministry of Public Instruction. She's constantly distressed by their poverty and their bare walls—when with gratitude her husband exclaims over their soup, she remains lost in fantasies of delicious dinners and gallant whispers. Though Mathilde does have one rich friend, a former schoolmate, she doesn't see her often, as doing so often makes her sad to return to her seemingly meager life.

One evening Monsieur Loisel comes home from work, triumphantly clutching an invitation to a lavish party at the Palace of the Ministry. Since he has thought Mathilde would be pleased by the news, he is confused by her crossness. When she explains that she cannot look forward to the occasion since she doesn't have a gown to wear to the ball, he asks her how much one might cost. When she tells him four hundred francs, he weakly agrees to sacrifice one of his own indulgences so that she might fulfill her fantasy of being the belle of the ball.

Though Mathilde finds a very beautiful gown, she remains anxious as the day of the ball draws near. When her husband inquires about the nature of her distress, she explains that she doesn't have a single piece of jewelry to wear with her gown. When her husband's first suggestion, that she wear some simple flowers, is dismissed, he urges her to borrow something from her rich friend, Madame Forestier. The next day at Madame Forestier's house, Mathilde is presented with a box containing many pieces of lavish jewelry. After trying on some ornaments before a mirror, she settles upon a superb diamond necklace.

The night of the ball is a great success—Mathilde is the most beautiful and elegant woman there—and all the men admire her as she dances with great fervor. Though Monsieur Loisel falls asleep in a deserted anteroom around midnight, she stays up enjoying herself until four o'clock in the morning. Then, finally, Monsieur Loisel throws common wraps over his wife's shoulders, and Mathilde insists they escape quickly, so as not to be seen by the other women.

When they arrive home, Mathilde removes her wraps so she might take one last wistful look at herself in the mirror. But upon seeing her reflection, she cries aloud—the necklace is gone! The husband and wife search frantically among the folds of her skirt, and soon after, Monsieur Loisel goes to retrace their steps on foot. He returns at seven o'clock in the morning, ashen-faced. To prolong an explanation, Mathilde tells Madame Forestier that she's broken the clasp on the piece and it is being repaired. The couple reports their loss to the police and the newspapers, but by the end of the week, they have lost all hope. They visit the jeweler whose name is on the loaned box, but he says he has not sold such a necklace. Finally, they find a necklace in a shop at the Palais Royal that looks exactly like it—though it costs forty thousand francs, they are given a bargain at thirty-six. Despite the extraordinary cost, Loisel unquestioningly spends all of his savings and resolves to borrow the rest.

From then on, Mathilde knows what it's like to be truly poor. She complains no longer, though, neither while she washes the linen nor when she bargains for her groceries. Monsieur Loisel takes a second job. Life continues in this way difficult way for ten years, until they finally have accumulated enough to pay back their debt. By this point, though, Mathilde looks old—strong, hard, and rough.

One Sunday on the Champs Elysées she runs into Madame Forestier, who doesn't recognize her; the reunion causes the vibrant, rich-looking woman to utter a cry about how much her friend has changed. Mathilde, overcome, explains that she had been relegated to a very difficult life because she's had to replace the lost necklace. Madame Forestier stops short and asks if the Loisels had bought a necklace of diamonds to replace hers. When Mathilde says yes, her friend, moved, takes her hands and carefully explains that the necklace was an imitation.

"The Necklace"

A clerk of modest means, **Monsieur Loisel** is so devoted to his wife that he delights in giving even small bits of the wealth she covets. When he brings home an invitation to the ball for the Ministry of Public Instruction, he allows her not only to get a dress but advises her to borrow a necklace from her friend. When the necklace is lost, he unquestioningly accepts full responsibility, spending all of his savings and borrowing the rest.

Despite being born to a family of clerks, **Mathilde Loisel's** overpowering desire for wealth and luxury causes her to resent her husband and the life they created together. Her fantasy seemingly comes true when she attends a ball in a new dress and a borrowed necklace, but when the necklace mysteriously disappears, she is forced to endure a life of poverty and sacrifice in order to pay for the one night of grandeur.

Though Mathilde usually resents visiting her wealthy friend because she comes home disappointed by her own lot in life, **Madame Forestier** graciously lends her a necklace to wear to the ball.

CRITICAL VIEWS ON
"The Necklace"

RICHARD FUSCO ON THE INVERSION STORY

[Richard Fusco is an assistant Professor of English at St. Joseph's University. He is the author of "Entrapment, Flight and Death: A Recurring Motif in Dickens with Plot and Interpretive Consequences for *Edwin Drood*," "On Primitivism in *The Call of the Wild*," and *Poe's Legacy for the Detective Story*. In this excerpt he examines Maupassant's use of the surprise ending and his repeated evocation of the theme of pride.]

By 1884, however, Maupassant mastered the intricacies of the inversion story and employed it repeatedly throughout the year. That year proved to be among his most productive, his published output totaling nearly sixty stories. With such demands upon his creativity, he found it necessary to repeat themes, symbols, and forms often, particularly those that were artistically and commercially successful. The surprise-inversion tactic probably appealed to Maupassant's sense of the dramatic. Recognizing its potential to play upon and appeal to his audience, he began to invoke it time and again throughout the year. Not yet concerned with the problem of amalgamating differing and, at times, conflicting literary forms, he produced stories that were thematically unified, relatively simplified, yet psychologically complicated, the result being perhaps the best examples of the subgenre ever written.

Certainly, the most famous of all these efforts was "La Parure" (1884, The Necklace). The surprise in the conclusion so overwhelming to the reader that often he tends to obliterate in his mind any other Maupassant story he has ever encountered. In nineteenth-century America, the literati seized upon it as an artistic blueprint. The author probably would have been amused and, in his strange way, gratified by the response the story would evoke: the same artistic devices would ultimately elicit both praise and censure.

Published early in 1884, "La Parure" demonstrates how the author had improved his technique. Unlike earlier efforts, Maupassant intimately tied the surprise with the complication of the story, and the bulk of the text explores the themes of pretension, vanity, and pride. Although Maupassant presents the protagonists in an irritating light, we can still sympathize with their plight, and consequently are able to partially identify with them. The ending attacks these human vices and, therefore, attacks our own values. By knitting these varied elements together with a finer stitch, then, he creates a stronger and more vivid fabric, capable of enduring in our literary memory.

At the heart of the short story is Mathilde Loisel's bourgeois aspiration. Choosing the easiest of all human foibles to attack—pride—Maupassant manipulates his audience so that it finds yearnings at first as insipid and selfish, later as tragic and possibly heroic. Pride exacerbates her supposition of poverty. It forces both material and psychological concessions from her acquiescent husband. He sacrifices his savings for a hunting weapon so that his wife may have a new dress for Minister Rampormeau's ball. But the dearly expensive dress symbolically pales before the elaborate diamond necklace she borrows from a wealthy friend. The jewelry thus encapsulates her pretension and pride, masking reality with her dream of what should have been. The party reinforces her delusion in that for one night everyone accepts her for what she pretends to be.

The loss of the necklace restores reality but does not end pride; it merely redirects it toward seemingly more productive ends. The Loisels secretly replace the lost jewels with a duplicate necklace, incurring an oppressive ten-year debt in the process. The repayment of these loans—yet another act of pride—reduces the couple to physical and emotional hardship. Mme. Loisel realizes true poverty by sacrificing the few luxuries she had but never appreciated fully. Regardless of our misgivings about her hauteur, we now pity her, rejudging her pride a virtue.

Maupassant subtly reinforces such sympathy through his characterization of M. Loisel. The husband is not only the victim of or the unwitting catalyst to his wife's pride; he too falls victim to the deadly sin. Although not directly responsible, he certainly contributes to the circumstances surrounding the loss of the necklace. It is he who suggests to his wife that she borrow the jewels from Jeanne Forestier, the wealthy friend. Come the crisis, however, his pride proves commensurate with that of his wife, for he is the one who resolves to replace the jewelry, a decision to which his wife accedes. By attributing the resolution to the more sympathetic husband, Maupassant manipulates us into believing that the couple's solution was indeed correct, especially since it complies with our Christian ethic.

Unlike earlier efforts when the surprise seemed divorced somewhat from character development, "La Parure" unites the inversion with the main theme by repeating that theme. Pride determined the decision to replace the necklace; it placed upon the couple a self-imposed vow of silence until they paid every debt. Once they had extricated themselves from their plight, however, pride once again inspires Mathilde to boast of her heroic sacrifice to her friend Jeanne upon their accidental meeting. Only then do we and Mme. Loisel discover that the lost necklace was composed of only false stones, that ten years of dissipating toil and pecuniary hardship were the product of a vainful miscalculation, that our vision itself was incorrect because it had been filtered by uninformed presumptions. In essence Maupassant has attacked our conceit about comprehending the perimeters of reality.

Granted, a good deal of Maupassant's small victory depends upon contrivance—most inversion stories do. Even sympathetic critics such as Steegmuller have some difficulty in resolving such awkwardness.[24] These artificial circumstances are, however, more acceptable in a short story than in longer fictional, forms. For example, the situation hinges upon the complementary personalities of the Loisels, which seem to conspire in aggravating their dilemma. Artistic economy dictates that the writer reveal only those traits of his characters that further the plot. Consequently, these characterizations may appear rather curt, approaching caricatures and leaving themselves subject to our dismissal as mere artifices designed to deceive.

Even the harshest of Maupassant's critics will admit, however, that the machinations in "La Parure" are tolerable amid the total impact of the story. Because of its brevity, we subconsciously permit the short story more leeway in achieving its artistic goal. Thus, we grant Maupassant's restricted portrayals of the Loisels as concessions toward unity.[25] Nevertheless, the unreality of their isolated pride paradoxically leads to our questioning our own assumptions about the wisdom of pride. By concentrating the story's impact at its conclusion, the surprise-inversion forces us to deal with the issue. Vial suggests that the absurdity of the Loisels' fate overwhelms our inclination to pity them.[26] "La Parure" does not end with Mme. Loisel's reaction to her friend's revelation. Such a passage would have risked directing a reader, through his empathy with the protagonist, toward a precise answer. By ending with the surprise Maupassant forces his audience to contend with its own perceptual folly. Indeed, the form elevates the importance of the inversion's effect upon the reader over that of any character. The resolution of our uncertainty continues the action of the story within "our" mind beyond the boundaries of the text.[27] It thus imprints a stronger image, so strong in the case of "La Parure" that it becomes for many a frame of reference by which to compare similar fiction.

Given the frequency that Maupassant used this story structure in 1884, it seems probable he recognized not only its potential but also that he had mastered it. Although each story deals with a differing subject, they all follow the same pattern. Unlike his earlier efforts, the 1884 inversion stories are so artfully constructed that every paragraph, every sentence, almost every noun and verb leads deceivingly to the surprise ending. Thus the significant moment becomes a target in the plot as well as a standard by which the author can determine the relevance of a description or characterization.

NOTES

24. *Maupassant: A Lion in the Path*, 204.

25. Sullivan would add that Maupassant scrupulously avoided assuming mystical powers of insight in his writings: "In a world where falsity masquerades as truth and blind chance rules, not even the clarity of the artist's eye is any guard against the deceptions and risks of life; all one can do is expose again and again the drama of deceit" (*Maupassant: The Short Stories*, 20).

26. *Guy de Maupassant*, 452.

27. For example, Dugan interestingly assumes as fact a reaction that Maupassant never described: "That moment of nothingness which the Loisels

experience upon the discovery of the truth about the necklace serves to reduce to futile meaninglessness the long tragic passing of years between the loss of the jewels and the revelation of their worthlessness" (*Illusion and Reality*, 158). In essence, the inversion has inspired Dugan to project his own response onto his perception of the Loisels.

> —Richard Fusco, *Maupassant and the American Short Story: The Influence of Form at the Turn of the Century*, (University Park, PA: The Pennsylvania State University Press, 1994): pp. 26–30.

STEPHEN LEACOCK ON THE INFLUENCE OF MAUPASSANT'S REALISM

[Stephen Leacock (1869–1944) was a Canadian humorist and political economist in the early twentieth century. He is the author of *Sunshine Sketches of a Little Town* and *Arcadian Adventures with the Idle Rich*. In this excerpt, taken from a compilation of Maupassant criticism, he cites "The Necklace" as most typical of Maupassant's influence on the art of storytelling.]

September 9, 1938

I consider that Guy de Maupassant's story *La Parure*—the most typical of his genius and method that I know—deserves to rank as a part of the history of the art of story telling—the purely objective method, excluding the sentiment of the author and refusing to sit down, and cry or laugh with his characters: in other words *realism* as we used to use the term when I was young. We used it as opposed to the romanticism of such writers as Charles Dickens, Hugo and Daudet, whose own feeling glowed warm in what they wrote, who coloured every character and action with their own feeling towards them.

But the realist in reality is pursuing an impossible ideal. You can't merely "state the facts", and in *selecting* them, even, you give colour to them. The basic idea of romanticism, the invitation to admiration or to tears or to laughter, is inherent in our minds: *expellas furco tamen usque recurrit*. The only correction that romanticism needs is as against trying to force sentiment, to announce it (l'afficher) when the narration doesn't substantiate it. Thus, in the province I know best, humor, it is no use saying that a situation is funny. You must make it funny; no use saying that "a roar of laughter greeted this witty sally", unless you make it witty. Otherwise the reader says, "Where does the sally come in?" In other words, the romanticist must not overtell his story. And within that limitation the realist will find that he is seeking the same effect.

Maupassant's work has long since been absorbed into our common inheritance, but that does not make it of less value.

—Stephen Leacock, "Inquiry Into His Present Fame," *Maupassant Criticism in France 1880–1940*, ed. Artine Artinian (New York, King's Crown Press, 1941): pp. 158–159.

JOHN RAYMOND DUGAN ON SETTING

[John Raymond Dugan is the author of *Notre Coeur: A Re-evaluation*. He cites here several stories in which Maupassant reduces the importance of setting in order to highlight a particular object, which, set apart from its typical physical context, becomes the narrative's focal point.]

Setting is frequently reduced in importance in Maupassant's short stories, yielding to a single object set apart from its physical context, and dominating the lives of the people concerned. And in many cases of this type the object itself is the title of the story. A list of these would include some of the author's best known works—"Les bijoux" (1883), "La parure" (1884), "Les épingles" (1888), "Le gâteau" (1882), "Le masque" (1889), "Le parapluie" (1884), and "La ficelle" (1883), to mention only some of the most popular. In every one, it is the object which is to mould the lives of the people and can even decide their fate. Poor Maitre Hauchecorne's whole existence is destroyed by that cursed piece of string which he innocently salvaged; the Loisel couple struggle to pay for the lost necklace; Monsieur Lantin only discovers his dead wife's infidelity through the presence of the jewels; and Monsieur Oreille's insecurity is intensified by that seemingly innocent umbrella. Much more than simply described, these objects take on a kind of life of their own, and speak by their very presence or absence (as is the case in "La parure") to their victims. They have far greater vitality than the famous "zaïmph" of Salammbô. And again the same contrast with Flaubert's technique is self-evident. Félicité's approach to life leads her inevitably and inexorably towards her parrot, whereas Maitre Hauchecorne and the Loisels are destroyed by the seemingly inert thing which increasingly controls their lives. Félicité bestows life on her parrot, whereas Maupassant's people are affected by things which take on a kind of independent vitality because of the unique relationship between them and their possessors. It is the fact that they are the possessors of a kind of life which indicates that Maupassant's position is veering away from a narrow and conventional determinism. The movement is not outward, drawing our attention to the object that instigates the conflict, but rather inward to the person affected by that object. They speak not of the person but to the person. Reality itself turns inward. Victims as these people inevitably are, they all struggle with their situation. If Maupassant finds himself in a corner, he is not going to abandon life without a fight.

—John Raymond Dugan, *Illusion and Reality: A Study of Descriptive Techniques in the Works of Guy de Maupassant*, (Paris: Mouton & Co., 1973): p. 26.

JOHN COWPER POWYS ON COARSENESS AND PREDATORY HUMOR

[John Cowper Powys (1872–1963) was a novelist, essayist, and poet. He is the author of studies on Rabelais and Dostoevsky and of novels including *Wolf Solent* and *Maiden Castle*. This extract focuses on Powys's admiration for Maupassant's unscrupulous depiction of human life in the grasp of animalistic wiles.]

It is idle to protest against the outrageous excursions of his predatory humour. The raw bleeding pieces—each, as one almost feels, with its own peculiar cry—of the living body of the world, clawed as if by tiger claws, are strange morsels for the taste of some among us. But for others, there is an exultant pleasure in this great hunt, with the deep-mouthed hounds of veracity and sincerity, after the authentic truth.

One touches here—in this question of the brutality of Guy de Maupassant—upon a very deep matter; the matter namely of what our pleasure exactly consists, as we watch, in one of his more savage stories, the flesh of the world's truth thus clawed at.

I think it is a pleasure composed of several different elements. The first of these is that deep and curious satisfaction which we derive from the exhibition in art of the essential grossness and unscrupulousness of life. We revenge ourselves in this way upon what makes us suffer. The clear presentation of an outrage, of an insult, of an indecency, is in itself a sort of vengeance upon the power that wrought it, and though it may sound ridiculous enough to speak of being avenged upon Nature, still the basic instinct is there, and we can, if we will, personify the immense malignity of things, and fancy that we are striking back at the gods and causing the gods some degree of perturbation; at least letting them know that we are not deceived by the illusions they dole out to us!

The quiet gods may well be imagined as quite as indifferent to our artistic vengeance as Nature herself, but at any rate, like the man in the Inferno who "makes the fig" at the Almighty, we have found vent for our human feelings. Another element in it is the pleasure we get—not perhaps a very Christian one, but Literature deviates from Christianity in several important ways—from having other people made fully aware, as we may be, of the grossness and unscrupulousness of life.

These other people may easily be assumed to be fidgety, meticulous, self-complacent purists; and as we read the short stories of Guy de Maupassant, we cannot resist calling up an imaginary company of such poor devils and forcing them to listen to a page of the great book of human judgment upon Nature's perversity.

Finally at the bottom of all there is a much more subtle cause for our pleasure; nothing less in fact than that old wild dark Dionysian embracing of fate, of fate however monstrous and bizarre, simply because it is there—an integral part of the universe—and we ourselves with something of that ingredient in our own heathen hearts. (…)

Guy de Maupassant visualises human life as a thing completely and helplessly in the grip of animal appetites and instincts. He takes what we call lust, and makes of it the main motive force in his vivid and terrible sketches. It is perhaps this very reason that his stories have such an air of appalling reality.

But it is not only lust or lechery which he exploits. He turns to his artistic purpose every kind of physiological desire, every sort of bodily craving. Many of these are quite innocent and harmless, and the denial of their satisfaction is in the deepest sense tragic. Perhaps it is in regard to what this word *tragic* implies that we find the difference between the brutality of Guy de Maupassant and the coarseness of the earlier English writers.

—John Cowper Powys, *Suspended Judgments: Essays on Books and Sensations*, (New York: G. Arnold Shaw, 1916): pp. 156–158, 159.

"A Piece of String"

This very short story, like "The Necklace," is all facts and circumstance—the flavor of the country market and the small but powerful agendas of those who inhabit the surrounding villages propel the narrative forward as the main character, Maitre Hauchecorne, attempts to fight back false branding as a thief.

When peasants who live in the countryside surrounding Goderville come into the village to shop, the men—dressed in their finest, though deformed from pushing their plows—often drag a cow or a calf by a rope. These animals are beaten by the men's wives, who, adorned in their shawls and head-wraps, walk more quickly and energetically. Market-day in Goderville is crowded and confusing, with the din of laughter and bargaining and the smell of milk, hay, and perspiration.

Into the confusion walks Maitre Hauchecorne of Breaute, who spies something on the ground. Since Maitre Hauchecorne is a true Norman, he assumes everything found can be of some use; ignoring his rheumatism, he stoops down to scoop up the bit of thin string. As he rolls up the string, he spots his nemesis, the harness-maker, Maitre Malandain, staring at him from his doorstep. Ashamed by having his enemy spot him picking up such a thing, he pretends to be looking for something else and finally escapes into the marketplace—his head bowed and his body bent over from rheumatic pain—and loses himself in the noise of the bargaining masses. Slowly the crowd thins out, and when at midday the Angelus strikes, those who have come from far away pour into the inns for lunch.

At Jourdain's the room is full of diners, and three spits are turning. Dishes laden with food are passed around while people exchange news of crops and affairs. Suddenly the noise of a drum beat in the yard summons all the customers to the door and windows, though their mouths are still full. The town crier informs the crowd that that very morning, on the Beuzeville road, Maitre Fortune Houlbreque of Mannville lost a black leather pocketbook containing five hundred francs and business papers.

Then the meal continues until everyone finishes their coffee, and a policeman walks in. He asks, "Is Maitre Hauchecorne, of Breaute, here?"

Maitre Hauchecorne identifies himself and follows the corporal to a place where the mayor is seated in an armchair. The mayor informs Hauchecorne that he was seen that morning on the Beuzeville road, picking up the pocketbook. The countryman is aghast and tells the mayor that he doesn't know anything about such a thing. The mayor informs him that Monsieur Malandain, the harness-maker, said he had seen him pick up the object.

Suddenly the old man understands, and presenting the evidence with a reddened face, he explains to the mayor that the harness-maker had seen him pick up a piece of string. The mayor shakes his head and explains that Monsieur Malandain's word can be relied upon; that there is no way the man could mistake a piece of string for a pocketbook. He adds that after the countryman was seen picking up the wallet, he even looked around in the mud to make sure no money had dropped from it.

Maitre Hauchecorne is embarrassed and afraid. Confronted by Malandain later, he hears the same testimony against him. After an hour, he requests to be searched, but nothing is found in his possession. Finally the mayor sends him away, warning that he will inform the public prosecutor.

Though Maitre Hauchecorne is free, by this point in the day, the news of his alleged guilt has spread. Upon leaving the mayor's office he is surrounded, interrogated, and ridiculed. He grows angry and feverish from others' doubt. When night falls and the time comes to return home, he leaves with three of his neighbors. On the way he points out the place on the road where he had picked up the piece of string. That evening he walks the village, making a point of telling everyone that he is innocent. He is met only by people who don't believe his tale.

The next day, Marius Paumelle, the farmhand of Maitre Breton, returns the pocket-book and its contents to Maitre Holbreque. The man says that he found the pocket-book on the road, but that since he didn't know how to read, he gave it to his master. As the news spreads, Maitre Hauchecorne becomes more and more excited that his innocence has been proven; he speaks of the resolution to his false accusation everywhere he goes. Still, people receive him without seeming convinced.

On the following Tuesday, he goes back to market with the need to tell his story. Malandain, standing on his doorstep, begins to laugh as he sees his enemy walk by. He accosts a farmer, who then punches him in the stomach and calls him a great rogue. Seated once again at Jourdain's, he begins to explain the entire affair, but he is heckled by people who insist that he must have returned the wallet himself in order to escape trouble. Unable to finish his meal, he leaves the table amidst jeers. He goes home confused and indignant, certain that it was impossible to prove his innocence.

So he begins again, still telling his tale, but this time adding more proofs and oaths every day. But the more vehemently he proclaims his innocence, the less he is believed. Behind his back, people insist that his elaborate explanations are "liar's proofs." Certain jokers make him tell the story of the piece of string in order to amuse themselves. Defeated, he slowly begins wasting away. By the end of December, he takes to his bed. He passes away in early January, and even on his deathbed he proclaims his innocence, repeating "A little piece of string—a little piece of string…"

"A Piece of String"

Hailing from Breaute, **Maitre Hauchecorne** is fastidious and economical. Like a true Norman, he believes that everything worth picking up could be of some use.

After a quarrel about a halter, **Maitre Malandain**, the harness-maker, continues to harbor a grudge against Maitre Hauchecorne. Having witnessed his nemesis stoop down to pick up something on the Beuzeville road, he suggests that Haucecorne is responsible for the missing wallet.

After Malandain reported seeing Maitre Hauchecorne pick up something in that very spot on the Beuzeville road where **Maitre Fortune Houlbreque of Mannville** said he lost his wallet, the mayor called in Maitre Hauchecorne for questioning.

A farmhand of Maitre Breton, **Marius Paumelle** returns the lost pocketbook to Maitre Holbreque of Manneville.

"A Piece of String"

JOHN GARDNER AND LENNIS DUNLAP ON SPECIFICITY AND RHYTHM IN THE SHORT STORY

[John Gardner is the author of *The Wreckage of Agathon*, *Grendel*, *The Sunlight Dialogues*, *Nickel Mountain*, *October Light*, and *Freddy's Book*. At the time of *The Forms of Fiction*'s publication, Lennis Dunlap was, with Gardner, a member of the English faculty at Chico State College. In this excerpt, they use Maupassant's "A Piece of String" in addition to Tolstoy's "Three Deaths" and Trilling's "Of This Time, Of That Place," to introduce the short story.]

The short story may have the form of a yam, sketch, fable, or tale; but it also has a more complex structure and less rigid adherence to convention. Like the tale, the short story uses characters, setting, and plot, and explores theme, but it differs from the tale in important respects: The short story is concerned with the world as it is, not as it should be; it has rhythmical and unified plot; and it is less limited by convention in its handling of point of view.

To say that the short story is concerned with the real world is not to say that the short story is always realistic. Like the tale and the fable, it may use symbolism. Maupassant's "A Piece of String," Tolstoy's "Three Deaths," and Lionel Trilling's "Of This Time, Of That Place" are all short stories; but one is strictly realistic—characters, setting, and action exist for their own sake—whereas two are, in different ways, symbolic—their meaning depends in part on symbolic relationships within the story or on symbolism established by reference to ideas outside the story. In "A Piece of String" the central character, Maître Hauchecorne, is a specific man with a specific problem: because he is known to be dishonest, he is assumed to be dishonest even when he is not. Maupassant does not in any way suggest within the story that Maître Hauchecorne represents all men or is similar to some specific man (a figure in myth, history, or contemporary politics, for example) or that the piece of string is more than a piece of string. The universality of the story is left to be inferred by the reader. (...)

In most short stories one finds rhythm, a more or less regular movement from one peak of tension to the next, steadily rising toward the tension of the major climax. In "A Piece of String" the first point of tension, or minor climax, comes when Maître Hauchecorne, picking up a piece of string, sees that he is observed by his enemy, Maître Malandain. Following a relaxation of tension, the story moves to a second point of climax with the public crier's revelation. A second relaxation of tension follows, then a third minor climax—Maître Hauchecorne's failure to convince the mayor or even his own neighbors that he did not find the missing purse. The purse is found and tension is relaxed; then comes the major climax of the story: even now that the purse has been found, Maître Hauchecorne's neighbors refuse to believe him.

—John Gardner and Lennis Dunlap, *The Forms of Fiction*, (New York: Random House, 1962): pp. 31, 33.

PERCY LUBBOCK ON THE ACT OF TELLING

[Percy Lubbock was a critic and editor and the author of *Roman Pictures*, *Earlham*, and *Samuel Pepys*. In this excerpt he lauds Maupassant's close eye for detail and his ability to place readers inside the scene unencumbered by authorial presence.]

In Maupassant's drama we are close to the facts, against them and amongst them. He relates his story as though he had caught it in the act and were mentioning the details as they passed. There seems to be no particular process at work in his mind, so little that the figure of Maupassant the showman is overlooked and forgotten as we follow the direction of his eyes. The scene he evokes is contemporaneous, and there it is, we can see it as well a he can. Certainly he is "telling" us things, but they are things so immediate, so perceptible, that the machinery of his telling, by which they reach us is unnoticed; the story appears to tell itself. Critically, of course, we know how far that is from being the case, we know with what judicious thought the showman is selecting the points of the scene upon which he touches. But the effect is that he is not there at all, because he is doing nothing that ostensibly requires any judgement, nothing that reminds us of his presence. He is behind us out of sight, out of mind; the story occupies us, the moving scene, and nothing else.

—Percy Lubbock, *The Craft of Fiction*, (New York: Viking, 1957), p. 113.

ANATOLE FRANCE ON MAUPASSANT'S NATIONALISM

[Anatole France, a novelist and critic, was the winner of the Nobel Prize for Literature in 1921. He is the author of, among other works, *La Rôtisserie de la Reine Pédauque* (*At the Sign of the Reine Pédauque*), *Les Dieux ont Soif* (*The Gods are Athirst*), and *La Révolte des Anges* (*The Revolt of the Angels*). In this excerpt France lauds Maupassant's feeling of order and economy and compares his work to the lifestyle of a good Norman landowner.]

"We have given M. Guy de Maupassant a fine enough retinue of story-tellers, ancient and modern. And it was but just. M. de Maupassant is one of the most whole-hearted story-tellers of this country in which so many and such good stories have been told. His strong, simple, and natural language has a flavour of the soil that makes us love him dearly. He possesses the three great qualities of the French writer, first, clearness, then again, clearness, and lastly, clearness. He has the feeling of proportion and order which is the feeling of our race. He writes as a good Norman landowner lives, with economy and joy. Sly, pawky, a good fellow, something of a boaster, a little foppish, ashamed of nothing but his large native kindliness, careful to hide what is most exquisite in his soul, full of sound sense, no dreamer, little curious of the things beyond the tomb, believing only what he sees, and reckoning only on what he touches, the man belongs to us, he is a fellow countryman. Hence the friendship which he inspires in everybody throughout France who can read.... He paints without hate and without love, without anger and without pity, the miserly peasants, drunken sailors, lost women, cheap clerks dazed by their toil, and all those humble beings whose humanity is as devoid of beauty as of virtue. He shows us all these grotesques and all these unfortunates so distinctly that we believe we see them before our eyes and find them more real than reality itself. He makes them live, but he does not judge them. We do not know what he thinks of those scoundrels, rogues, and blackguards whom he has created and who haunt us. He is a skilful artist, and he knows that he has done all that is needed when he has given life.

—Anatole France. *On Life and Letters*. Trans. A.W. Evans. (Freeport, NY: Books for Libraries Press, 1971): pp. 46–47.

Joseph Conrad on Maupassant's Allegiance to Facts

[Joseph Conrad, often considered one of the greatest English novelists, is the author of *Heart of Darkness*, *Typhoon*, *Nostromo*, and *Under Western Eyes*. Here he commends Maupassant's ability to remain true to facts and resist the attraction to write towards personal gratification or to alleviate loneliness.]

Except for his philosophy, which in the case of so consummate an artist does not matter (unless to the solemn and naïve mind), Maupassant of all writers of fiction demands least forgiveness from his readers. He does not require forgiveness because he is never dull.

The interest of a reader in a work of imagination is either ethical or that of simple curiosity. Both are perfectly legitimate, since there is both a moral and excitement to be found in a faithful rendering of life. And in Maupassant's work there is the interest of curiosity and the moral of a point of view consistently preserved and never obtruded for the end of personal gratification. The spectacle of this immense talent served by exceptional faculties triumphing over the most thankless subjects by an unswerving singleness of purpose is in itself an admirable lesson in the power of artistic honesty, one may say of artistic virtue. The inherent greatness of the man consists in this, that he will let none of the fascinations that beset a writer working in loneliness turn him away from the straight path, from the vouchsafed vision of excellence. He will not be led into perdition by the seductions of sentiment, of eloquence, of humour, of pathos; of all that splendid pageant of faults that pass between the writer and his probity on the blank sheet of paper, like the glittering cortege of deadly sins before the austere anchorite in the desert air of Thebaide. This is not to say that Maupassant's austerity has never faltered; but the fact remains that no tempting demon has ever succeeded in hurling him down from his high, if narrow, pedestal.... He refrains from setting his cleverness against the eloquence of the facts. There is humour and pathos in these stories; but such is the greatness of his talent, the refinement of his artistic conscience, that all his high qualities appear inherent in the very things of which he speaks, as if they had been altogether independent of his presentation. Facts, and again facts are his unique concern. That is why he is not always properly understood. His facts are so perfectly rendered that, like the actualities of life itself, they demand from the reader that faculty of observation which is rare, the power of appreciation that is generally wanting in most of us who are guided mainly by empty phrases requiring no effort, demanding of us no qualities except a vague susceptibility to emotion. Nobody had ever gained the vast applause of a crowd by the simple and clear exposition of vital facts. Words alone strung upon a convention have fascinated us as worthless glass beads strung on a thread have charmed at all times our brothers the unsophisticated savages of the islands. Now, Maupassant, of whom it has been said that he is a master of the *mot juste*, has never been a dealer in words. His wares have been, not glass beads, but polished gems;

not the most rare and precious, perhaps, but of the very first water after their kind....

Maupassant's renown is universal, but his popularity is restricted. It is not difficult to perceive why. Maupassant is an intensely national writer. He is so intensely national in his clearness, in his aesthetic and moral conceptions that he has been accepted by his countrymen without having had to pay the tribute of flattery either to the nation as a whole, or to any class, sphere, or division of the nation. The truth of his art tells with an irresistible force; and he stands excused from the duty of patriotic posturing. He is a Frenchman of Frenchmen beyond question or cavil, and with that he is simple enough to be universally comprehensible (…)

His qualities, to use the charming and popular phrase, are not lovable … It is evident that Maupassant looked upon his mankind in another spirit than those writers who make haste to submerge the difficulties of our holding place in the universe under a flood of false and sentimental assumptions. Maupassant was a true and dutiful lover of our earth. He says himself in one of his descriptive passages: "Nous autres que seduit la terre." … It was true. The earth for him had a compelling charm. He looks upon her august and furrowed face with the fierce insight of real passion. His is the power of detecting the one immutable quality that matters in the changing aspects of nature and under the ever-shifting surface of life. To say that he could not embrace in his glance all its magnificence and all its misery is only to say that he was human. He lays claim to nothing that his matchless vision has not made his own. This creative artist has the true imagination; he never condescends to invent anything; he sets up no empty pretences. And he stoops to no littleness in his art— least of all to the miserable vanity of a catching phrase.

—Joseph Conrad, "Guy de Maupassant." (London: Thomas J. Wise, 1919): pp. 1–2.

"The Horla"

First published as a short story in 1886, "The Horla" is an example of some of Maupassant's stories—among them "The Fear," "Apparition," and "The Death"—centered on incomprehensible occurrences and terrifying sensations. Biographers speculate that the author's insecurity about life's purpose and his hallucinations of having a double inspired him to write in this genre.

The series of journal entries which comprise the story begin May 8, when the unnamed narrator comments joyfully on his country, his town, and his house. Around eleven o'clock in the morning, a line of boats passes by, including a Brazilian three-master, which he saluted.

A few days later the narrator reports a slight feverish attack and says he feels low-spirited. He postulates that the air is full of mysterious forces and attempts to make sense of the fact that he'll wake up happy, but then, after going down to the water, he returns chilled and upset. The mystery of the "Invisible" is profound, he says.

Beginning on May 16, the next several entries describe the narrator's increasing sense of fever and impending danger. He reflects with disbelief on how well he had felt a few weeks earlier. He consults his doctor, who finds no serious symptoms, aside from a quickened pulse and dilated eyes. He says that when he tries to read, he cannot make sense of the letters. After locking his bedroom door, he looks under the bed and listens for strange noises, waiting for sleep the way one might wait for an executioner. He only can rest for a few hours before he is seized by a nightmare that someone is coming for him.

On June 2 the narrator reports that his condition is worsening and that the doctor's suggestions have no effect. One day, enroute to La Bouille in an attempt to get fresh air, he feels a sudden shiver come over him, along with the sense he's being followed. He turns around suddenly and finds he is alone. He then sits down bewildered, forgetting how he has come.

A month later, the narrator reports that he's feeling quite

cured after returning from a trip to Mont Saint-Michel, where, accompanied by a monk, he climbed to the top of a hill and entered a beautiful, Gothic church. There the monk said the country people believe that at night they can hear people talking and goats bleating. When the narrator asks him if he believes such stories, the monk poses a question in response: "Do we see the hundred-thousandth part of what exists?" The narrator wonders if the monk is a philosopher or perhaps a fool.

The next day, however, the narrator reports having slept badly; the coachman has described a similar spell having come over him. By July 4 his old nightmares have returned, and the narrator says he feels as though someone was sucking his life out from between his lips. On July 5 the narrator reports seeing an empty glass and an empty bottle of water after witnessing both items full a few hours earlier. By July 6 he wonders if he is in fact going mad, if he might be drinking his water in the middle of the night without knowing it.

On July 10 he recounts the story from a few evening experiments with a series of foodstuffs on his table. A night earlier he put water and milk on his table, wrapping up the bottles in white muslin and rubbing his lips, beard, and hands with pencil lead before retiring for the evening. After a typically fitful night's sleep he rushes to see what had happened and is horrified to find both the milk and the water drained, despite the muslin being entirely intact. He resolves to leave for Paris immediately.

On July 12, from Paris, he reports that he must be going mad, if not a somnabulist. After doing some errands he ends up watching a play. Such stimulation completed his cure, he thinks, concluding that too much solitude is dangerous for active minds.

On July 14, Bastille Day, the narrator reflects upon the oddness of a government-sanctioned celebration, and on July 16 he reports witnessing a strange and disturbing occurrence while dining at the home of his cousin, Madame Sable. Another guest, Doctor Parent, began explaining his involvement with experiments of hypnotism and offered to try his technique on the narrator's cousin. As Doctor Parent hypnotized the woman, he instructed her to awaken at eight o'clock the next morning and ask the narrator for five-thousand francs. The narrator explains he was skeptical, as he'd known his cousin for a long while. The next morning, however, at half-past eight, Madame Sable enters, begging for five thousand francs. When the narrator explains that he does not have them at his disposal, she begins to despair. Finally, the narrator concedes to give up the money, and only then does he remind his cousin about the hypnotism. Madame Sable has no recollection of such an order, and after she returns to Doctor Parent that afternoon to be hypnotized once more, she no longer remembers asking her cousin for the money.

Back at home, nothing seems especially amiss until on August 4 the narrator reports quarrels among the servants, who declare that the glasses have been broken in the cupboards at night. On August 6 the narrator concludes he's mad, having seen a flower raise itself from a bush and remain suspended in the air. In an entry the following day he wonders if a profound disturbance must have entered his brain and affected the logic of his thoughts. He considers these things as he walks by the side of the water, thinking that an unknown force has seized him and is continually calling him back to his home. During the next few entries he reflects that he's lost all self-control—on August 14, for example, he remembers being seized by an inexplicable need to eat strawberries. On August 16, he goes to the library and begs to borrow Dr. Herrmann Herestauss's treatise on the unknown inhabitants of the ancient and modern world. As he gets into his carriage, though he means to give directions to the railway station, something seizes him and causes him to bid the carriage driver to take him home.

He next reports that after reading until one o'clock in the morning, he's found nothing in Herestauss to explain the demon which haunts him. He falls asleep, and after dreaming for three quarters of an hour, he awakens to find the pages of his book turning on their own. Rising from his bed with the intent to somehow seize the invisible beast, the narrator knocks over his chair and frightens the demon away from him. On August 19 the narrator reports reading in the "Revue du Monde Scientifique" that an epidemic of madness is raging in the Province of San-Paulo. He remembers the Brazilian three-master passing him and concludes that the reign of man has ended and that another beast has arrived. As he reflects, he says "I fancy that he is shouting out his name to me and I do not hear him—the yes…. I cannot—repeat—it—Horla—I have heard—the Horla." Only then does he remember the words of the monk and Mont Saint-Michel. He wonders that since there are so few stages of development of man, why shouldn't there be one more? He concludes to kill the Horla who haunts him.

On August 20 the narrator pretends to be writing in order to deceive the invisible demon. Suddenly he feels the Horla watching him, standing over him, practically touching his ear. Looking in the mirror, he sees him, and even as he looks away, the horror remains. On August 22 he sends for iron shutters for his room.

On September 10 the narrator writes from the Hotel Continental in Rouen. He reports that after having waited with the house open all night, he sensed the Horla around him and fastened the iron shutters. Running downstairs to the drawing room he took the two lamps and poured oil all over the carpet—after setting fire to it he escaped, hid at the bottom of the garden, and watched his house burn. Suddenly, overwhelmed with horror, he runs to the village screaming "Fire!" By the time he gets help, he returns to see the house as nothing but a huge funeral pyre and wonders if the Horla is in there, dead.

But what if he is not dead? wonders the narrator. Perhaps time alone can affect this being. Suddenly there is no doubt in the narrator's mind that the Horla is still alive. He resolves then, with complete conviction, to kill himself.

"The Horla"

Wondering from the outset of the story about the elusive forces that effect happiness and disillusion, **the Narrator** feels his sanity slip from his grasp after a Brazilian three-master passes by him one sunny May day. As the story progresses, his journal entries become more desperate and searching; after he burns his house down in an attempt to rid himself from that which plagues him, he concludes that the only way out of his predicament is to kill himself.

After a few weeks of feeling strange and ill, the narrator approaches his **doctor**, who pronounces him in good health, aside from an elevated pulse and dilated eyes. The doctor prescribes a course of shower baths and a bromide of potassium.

On a trip to Mont Saint-Michel the narrator encounters a **monk** who tells him the country people think that at night one can hear talking going on beneath the sand. When the narrator wonders aloud if such legends could possibly be true, the monk asks him, "Do we see the hundred-thousandth part of what exists?"

When staying in Paris for a few days the narrator has dinner with his cousin, **Madame Sable**. After being hypnotized by one of the other guests, Madame Sable asks the narrator for five thousand francs. When the hypnotism is reversed the following day, she has no recollection of her request.

The husband of one of Madame Sable's female guests, **Doctor Parent** explains his interest in experimenting with hypnotism. Although the narrator expresses his disbelief, Doctor Parent's successful hypnotism of Madame Sable silences him.

A Doctor of Philosophy and Theogony, **Dr. Hermann Herestauuss** wrote the history and manifestation of invisible beings which hover around man. Though the narrator picks up his treatise, he cannot find an explanation for his affliction.

After concluding that the reign of man is over and that a new power has overtaken the earth, the narrator listens to a call and determines that the name of this new and all-powerful creature is the **Horla**.

"The Horla"

JOAN C. KESSLER ON THE INVISIBLE BEING

[Joan C. Kessler is editor of the collection *Night Shadows: Twentieth Century Stories of the Uncanny*. Here, in the introduction to the short story collection *Demons of the Night*, she gives background to Maupassant's preoccupation with the supernatural and explains the influence of Eduard von Hartmann's *Philosophie des Unbewussten*, which is mentioned in "The Horla."]

The theme of the Invisible Being, most fully developed in "Le Horla" ("The Horla"), 1887, epitomizes Maupassant's preoccupation with the "other side" of the positivist coin: a nagging disquietude about the invisible, intangible dimension of reality that remains inaccessible to empirical investigation. This brooding concern would explain the writer's obsession with the phenomena of magnetism and hypnosis, which suggest the existence of forces hovering just beyond human understanding. (...)

Throughout the centuries, as the hypnotist Docteur Parent remarks to the narrator of "The Horla," man's fear of what lay beyond his senses took the form of a superstitious belief in the supernatural, until "Mesmer ... opened up for us an unexpected path, and, during the last four or five years in particular, we have ... arrived at some remarkable results." (...)

A book that attracted a sizable audience in the last decades of the century in France was Eduard von Hartmann's *Philosophie des Unbewussten* (1868; French translation in 1877). The term "unconscious," in Hartmann's usage, has a metaphysical as well as biological dimension. Like the Schopenhauerian "will," it designates the impersonal force of nature which compels individuals to obey instinctual drives (while often cloaking them in idealistic disguise) in order to advance the larger goals of the species. Although Sigmund Freud was later to give it a more "scientific" and systematic treatment in the context of human psychology, it is nonetheless true that by the 1870s and 1880s, the general notion of the unconscious had become a commonplace in Europe. Maupassant was one of the writers in late nineteenth-century France who would give this theme powerfully compelling literary form. The phantasm that ensnares the hapless protagonist of "The Horla" is a force which—*within us*—is both us and not as, a force which makes us a stranger to ourselves. Maupassant's narrator expresses a striking intuition:

> [W]ithout knowing it, I was living that mysterious double life that makes us wonder if there are two beings within us, or if an alien being, invisible and unknowable, momentarily animates (when our soul is benumbed) our captive body which obeys the other as it does our own self, more than our own self.

The metaphor of the unknown visitor, who takes over not only a person's house and home but his entire being, is linked thematically with the mirror symbolism in Maupassant's tale: the protagonist, unable to perceive himself in the glass, is convinced that the Horla is hiding his reflection. In a metaphor familiar to German romanticism, losing one's reflection is equivalent to losing one's soul. Maupassant's use of this troubling motif only reinforces the reader's impression of a man who has become radically alienated from his own self: in a concrete and explicit fashion, his "self" has become "other." For the author, it was the gradual onset of madness which brought this sense of alienation to a harrowing pitch of intensity. Maupassant confided to his friend Paul Bourget that often, upon returning home, he would fall prey to a hallucinatory encounter with his double, seated in his own chair. Elsewhere he recounts a terrifying experience of self-estrangement which has a mirror as its focal point:

Do you know that when I stare for a while at my own image reflected in a mirror, I have sometimes felt myself losing the notion of the ego? At these moments everything grows confused in my mind and I find it strange to be looking at a face that is no longer familiar to me. Then it seems peculiar that I should be what I am.... And I feel that if this condition were to last a minute longer, I would go completely mad. Little by little, all thought would empty out of my brain.

> —Joan C. Kessler, *Demons of the Night: Tales of the Fantastic, Madness, and the Supernatural from Nineteenth-Century France*, (Chicago, The University of Chicago Press, 1995): pp. xlii–xliii, xliv–xlvi.

NANCY H. TRAILL ON FIRST-PERSON NARRATION

[Nancy H. Traill is a Professor of Humanities at York University, Ontario. In this extract she illustrates the way in which first-person narration, a frame, and other stylistic techniques add to Maupassant's fantastic tales, specifically "The Horla."]

Stylistically, the narrator's discourse parallels the gradual increase in the intensity of his experience. It is also an indicator of the ways in which his theory changes. For instance, when he sees a rose apparently being picked and held suspended, his words are, 'j'ai vu' (2: 927). The absence of a grammatical object suggests that the narrator cannot yet identify what he has seen; he is simply voicing his awareness of an alien presence. During the most vivid of his experiences, when he 'sees' the Horla, he exclaims: 'je l'ai vu!' (2: 935), the grammatical object referring to a specific and individualized entity. At a certain point, he accumulates nouns and related verbs, an act that represents his effort to concretize and give expression to his experience. Before he sees the Horla, he knows it by its influence: 'Someone is in command of all my actions, all my movements, all my thoughts

[…]' (2: 929). Afterwards, his utterances express an aggressive desire to counter the Horla's influence by asserting his own will. It has become for him a concrete being upon which he can act: 'I would have the strength of the desperate, I would have my hands, my knees, my chest, my forehead, my teeth to strangle him, crush him, bite him, tear him apart' (2: 935; B36).

The description of the Horla itself is semantically indefinite, conveyed indirectly in similes and figurative language: 'It was as bright as day, yet I could not see myself in my mirror! […] Then, all of a sudden, I began to make myself out in a mist at the back of the mirror, as though through a sheet of water […] it was like the end of an eclipse' (2: 935–6; B37). The obliqueness of his language—it is almost entirely made up here of metaphors—is a mirror of his experience. The narrator has perceived the Horla indirectly. The Horla's 'opaque transparency' [transparence opaque] finds its echo in the symbol most frequently associated with it, the colour white. The narrator deduces that the creature arrived on a white Brazilian three-master and was attracted to his white house; his own experiment revealed that the Horla would drink only water (transparent) or milk (white) (2: 920).

The opening of the narrative is strongly contrasted with the dramatic events that follow. In the first episode, calmly descriptive, the protagonist is at one with nature: 'What a lovely day! I spent the whole morning stretched out in the grass in front of my house under the enormous plane tree that covers it, sheltering it and shading it completely' (2: 913; B38). Compare the style of the climactic 19 August entry, which is highly charged, dramatic, and presents the event in all its emotionality and immediacy; abrupt syntactic phrases contribute to the discursive tension: 'I'm done for!' (2: 929); 'It's he, he, the Horla […] He is inside me, he's becoming my soul; I'll kill him!' (2: 935). Despite the affectivity of such passages, the narrator's logical coherence shows no sign of deteriorating and there is no trace of pathological semantic or syntactic distortion. The texture of his discourse speaks strongly for the narrator's sanity.

In the crucial 19 August entry, stylistic contrast recurs in the narrator's description of his room. His nonchalant and impersonal tone in itemizing his furniture tells us how banal is the setting for this most remarkable experience: 'In front of me, my bed, an old oak four-poster; on the right, my fireplace; on the left, my carefully closed door [...]' (2: 935; B39). It is a bald description, preceded by a flood of verbs expressing violent action (strangle, crush, bite, tear apart). He seems to get a grip on himself until he observes that his reflection is missing, with the Horla's interposition between him and the mirror. This brings him back to the exclamatory style: 'It was empty, bright to the very depths, full of light!' Another slowly paced description follows, as the narrator describes just what he does see in the mirror: 'it seemed to me that this [sheet of] water was slowly creeping from left to right, making my reflection more distinct moment by moment' (2: 936; B40). At the end of the entry the narrator resumes his emotionally charged style, and the circle, stylistically, is closed (2: 936). Interestingly, the shift in register in the 19 August entry is signalled by different tenses of the same verb: 'and I pretended that I was writing' ['et je fis semblant d'écrire'] 'so I was pretending to write' ['donc je faisais semblant d'écrire']. The simple past and the conjunction of the first phrase mark a completed action which took place the evening before and which is being viewed from the narrating present. The second is introduced by 'donc,' which connotes here not consequence, but the picking up of the narrative thread which was retarded while the narrator itemized his furniture. The imperfect 'faisais' brings the past into the present, as though relived, and makes more immediate the event that follows—seeing the Horla. The entry as a whole is similarly enframed, opening with 'I saw him!' ['je l'ai vu!'] and closing with 'I have seen him' ['je l'avais vu'].

The mirror itself, in the 19 August entry, is marked by stylistic shifts and textural density: from 'armoire à glace' to 'ma glace,' from 'grand verre limpide' to 'miroir.' 'Armoire à glace' is stylistically neutral and simply denotes one of the items of furniture in the narrator's room; 'ma glace' is personalized by the possessive pronoun. Significantly, he uses the pronoun at the moment when he is most at a loss; that is, when he notices that his reflection is missing. 'Grand verre limpide' is the narrator's poetic expression when confronting the enigma, helpless and unable to move. 'Miroir,' however, literalizes a metaphor ('au fond du miroir') for a unique effect. The narrator progresses from the mirror as an object that occupies a certain space in his room to the mirror *as* space; that is, the virtual or illusory space which we see in the mirror. It is in this *illusion* of space, paradoxically, that the invisible becomes visible. The opposition corresponds to the expressions 'glace vide' and 'verre limpide,' which serve as a prelude to his phrase 'transparence opaque.' This episode is a stylistic mise-en-abîme that mimics the larger, surrounding, episode of the narrator's encounter with the Horla.

Questions ('what's the matter with me?' ['qu'ai je donc?']; 'so close that I could perhaps touch him, seize him?' ['si près que je pourrais peut-être le toucher, le saisir?'], etc.) are a stylistic feature of Maupassant's fantastic tales and index even some of his titles. Obviously they serve a purpose, expressing his protagonists' uncertainty, their desire to make sense of bewildering events. In 'The Horla,' the questions have a very clear semantic function: the narrator's shuttling back and forth from question to answer represents his obsessive querying of a reality grown unfamiliar, his struggle to 'plug the gap' (Dentan 1976, 46) in a paranormal fictional world where the unknown intrudes and must be expected.

First-person narration, the enframed narrative, syntactic and stylistic devices signifying what can only be called shattered nerves—these are features of Maupassant's fantastic tales that he used no less frequently in his realistic works. Maupassant's entire oeuvre, MacNamara observes, is 'founded on an aesthetic of rupture,' a 'nervousness of style' to be identified with the fictional language of Realism in general (1986, 196).

—Nancy H. Traill, *Possible Worlds of the Fantastic: The Rise of the Paranormal in Fiction*, (Toronto: University of Toronto Press, 1996): 129–132.

JANKO LAVRIN ON INTROSPECTION

[Janko Lavrin is the author of *A First Series of Representative Russian Stories: Pushkin to Gorky, Russian Writers: Their Lives and Literature*, and studies on Tolstoy and Gorky. In this extract he uses Chekhov as a comparison and connects Maupassant's actual suffering to his preoccupation, in writing, with the "riddle of the universe."]

An incurable pessimist on the one hand, and a sensuous Epicurean on the other, Maupassant looks upon the world as a stage which, being both disgusting and amusing, provides at least plenty of raw material for his writings. Who does not know and admire the polish of those writings, which often are as clear and also as cold as a crystal? But if we dive beneath the surface of his work, we can perhaps find out what his coldness must have cost him. He needed a great deal of forced indifference, of cynical irony and self-assertive spirit in order to conceal the secret that he, too, had a warm heart, and a soul whose wings had been clipped before its very first flight. He confesses—though rarely— in his more intimate works and letters, how much he had suffered from life, and how misleading his cold exterior often was. Here are a few passages from a letter to P. Neveux:

"Thinking becomes an abominable torture, when the whole of my brain is nothing but one wound. There is so much pain (*tant de meurtrissure*) in my head that every stir of my ideas makes me want to cry. Why? Why? Dumas would say that I have a heart which is both proud and shy (*honteux*): a human heart, the ancient human heart at which one may laugh, but which all the same gets stirred and makes us suffer. Intellectually, too, I have a Latin soul which is much battered. And then, there are days when I do not think and nevertheless suffer, because I am of the sensitive ones (*car je suis de la famille des écorchés*). But as for this, I never tell nor show it; I even believe that I manage splendidly to conceal it. I am sure other people think I am one of the coldest men on earth. But I am only a sceptic, which is not the same; I am a sceptic because. my sight is clear. And my eyes say to my heart: 'Hide yourself. old friend, you are ridiculous!' And it hides itself." (…)

His later introspective period was almost bound to lead him from the riddle of the human soul to the riddle of the universe. Although a materialist at heart, Maupassant became more and more haunted by the irrational side of life. Partly owing to his disease—he began to suffer quite early, at the age of thirty-three, from hallucinations, from division of personality, and also from terrible symbolic dreams and delusions which brought his imagination into contact, as it were, with a new and mysterious dimension. The consumptive Chekhov had some "pathologic" glimpses of a similar kind, which he recorded in his *Black Monk*. But what a difference between the unearthly exaltations of Chekhov's consumptive visionary and the unfathomable terror of *Le Horla*, of *Lui*, and others, a terror which becomes even stronger by virtue of the lucid concreteness of Maupassant's style and language.

It was his psychological introspection on the one hand, and his disease on the other, that gradually brought Maupassant nearer to the Unknown and fostered his interest in the irrational aspects of existence. It was at this stage that he began to crave also for a deeper, more universal, more spiritual art.

—Janko Lavrin, Studies in European Literature, (London: Constable & Company Limited, 1929): pp. 183–184, 186–187.

ERNEST GEORGE ATKIN ON THE PSYCHOLOGY OF SUPERNATURALISM

[In this excerpt Ernest George Atkin studies "The Horla" narrator's failed attempt to make sense of his situation, which mirrors other misguided quests. Atkin rationalizes the narrator's conclusion at the end, that man is not the last stage of Evolution.]

Using the same introspective method, *Le Horla* develops a psychology of supernaturalism commensurate with the utmost emotional and logical scope of the author's idea of fear. The helpless narrator of *Lui?*, knowing that he did not exist, yet unable to reason himself out of the fear that would assail him when he was alone, felt that his only salvation lay in companionship. The "halluciné raîsonnant" of the later story pushes his feverish analysis to a point where subjective manifestations become, to his distraught mind, objective proof of the existence and the unseen presence of a Being with superhuman powers. And with the discovery that he is dominated by the tyrannous "Horla" comes the crushing realization that his own existence—in time all human existence even—is doomed; suicide alone will release him. The successive stages of his introspection are more numerous and more searching than in *Lui?*. They deal with his fear in connection with nightmare, somnambulism, hypnotism and hallucination; the brooding fear that he may be going mad compels self-examination and an analysis of madness; refusing to believe that his senses have deceived him, he makes a supreme effort to reconcile the mysterious manifestations with the laws of reason and nature; he inquires into the cause of all supernatural beliefs and fears. As he surveys the mass of traditional superstitions, he sees in all these inventions the straining of human intelligence to penetrate a mysterious Unknown, to comprehend an unseen Presence of which men have always been conscious. He sees reason fatally handicapped by wretchedly inadequate powers of perception; imagination, ever prone to create frightful mysteries and supernatural agencies in the face of something unexplained. Hence the popular belief in the supernatural, hence the crude stories of ghosts and demons as well as the equally childish conceptions of God. And now when science, with more sophisticated intelligence, ventures upon the mysterious ground of hypnotism, suggestion and the like, we feel the shadow of the same unseen Presence. What are all these phenomena but signs of its hidden power, which to our own peril we try to control? This view, he argues further, is confirmed by evolution. Why should man be the final stage? Why not a new and superior Being, more perfect than our feeble nature, a superhuman Being that is invisible simply because our sight is weak? Thus reasoning, this victim of tortured imagination. and sensibility is driven to a paradoxical conclusion and a psychological *impasse*, his explanation, so far from explaining away his fear, plunges him into greater terror than ever. This is a result which accords fully with the author's guiding principle. The nature of the thing called the Horla is, by definition, unknowable in any ordinary sense, and must therefore continue to terrify. The terror is greater than that of *Lui?* because the mystery is greater. The half-materialized phantom of that story was directly traceable to an hallucination. The Horla, less tangible but endowed with a more formidable personality, is symbolic not of a particular mystery like hallucination but of the mysteriousness of universal, ultimate reality—the reality that lies beyond the reach of our perception. In the light of Maupassant's previous supernaturalism, this impressive creation is clearly nothing less than the imaginative concrete personification of his abstract Unknown, of his *"ce qu'on ne comprend pas"* in its widest signification.

—Ernest George Atkin, "The Supernaturalism of Maupassant," *PMLA* 42, no. 1 (1927), pp. 205–207.

Guy de Maupassant

"La Main d'ecorche," 1875.

L'Histoire du vieux temps, 1879.

"Une fille," 1880.

"Boule de Suif," 1880.

La Maison Tellier, 1881.

Une Vie, 1882.

Au Soleil, 1884.

Bel-Ami, 1885.

Mont-Oriol, 1886.

Pierre et Jean, 1888.

"Le Roman," 1888.

Sur l'eau, 1888.

Fort comme la mort, 1889.

La Vie errante, 1890.

Notre Coeur, 1890.

Musotte, 1891.

Guy de Maupassant

Barrows, S., *Distorting Mirrors: Visions of the Crowd in Late Nineteenth-Century France*. New Haven, CT: Yale University Press, 1981.

Becker, George. *Documents of Modern Literary Realism*. Princeton: Princeton University Press, 1963.

Bloom, Harold. *The Anxiety of Influence*. Oxford: Oxford University Press, 1973.

Coulter, S., *Damned Shall Be Desire*. London: Cape, 1958.

Cox, Roy Alan. "Dominant Ideas in the Works of Guy de Maupassant," University of Colorado Studies, 19 (1932): 77–157.

Croce, Benedetto. "Maupassant," *European Literature in the Nineteenth Century*, trans. Douglas Ainslee. New York: Knopf, 1924: 344–58.

Donaldson-Evans, Mary K. "The Imaginary Universe of Guy de Maupassant." Ph.D. thesis, University of Pennsylvania, 1975. *DAI* 36 (1976): 8093A.

Dumesnil, Rene. *Guy de Maupassant*. Paris: Armand Colin, 1933.

Faverty, Frederic. *Your Literary Heritage*. Philadelphia: Lippincott, 1959.

Freimanis, Dzintars. "Maupassant as Romantic." *Romanic Review* 54 (1963): 274–80.

Gordon, Carol. *The House of Fiction*. New York: Charles Scribner's Sons, 1950.

Hainsworth, G.H. "Pattern and Symbol in the Work of de Maupassant." *French Studies* 5, no. 1 (Jan 1951) 1–17.

Harris, Trevor A. Le V., "Repetition in Maupassant: Irony as Originality?" *Forum for Modern Language Studies* 25, no. 3 (July 1989): 265–75.

Hearn, Lafcadio. *Essays in European and Oriental Literature*. Freeport, NY: Books for Libraries Press, 1968.

Ignotus, Paul. *The Paradox of Maupassant*. London, Ontario: London University Press, 1966.

James, Henry. *Partial Portraits*. London: Macmillan, 1888.

Killick, F., "Family Likeness in Flaubert and Maupassant: 'La Legende de Saint Julien l'Hospitalier' and 'Le Donneur d'eau denite,'" *Forum for Modern Language Studies* 24 no. 4 (Oct 1988).

Lemoine, Fernand. *Maupassant*. Paris: Editions Universitaires, 1957.

Lerner, Michael. *Maupassant*. New York: George Braziller, Inc., 1975.

Lumbroso, A. *Souvenirs sur Maupassant*. Rome: Bocca, 1905.

Matthews, J.H., "Things in the Naturalist Novel." *French Studies* 14 (1960): 212–23.

Moger, A.S., "Narrative Structure in Maupassant: Frames of Desire", *Publications of the Modern Language Association* 100, no. 3 (May 1985): 315–27.

———, "That Obscure Object of Narrative," *Yale French Studies* 63, (1982): 129–38.

Neveux, Pol., "Guy de Maupassant," Introduction to *Boule de Suif*. Paris: Conard, 1908.

O'Faolain, Sean. *The Short Story*. New York: Devin-Adair, 1951.

Pasco, Allan H. "The Evolution of Maupassant's Supernatural Stories." *Symposium* 23 (1969): 150–9.

Raoul, V. *The French Fictional Journal*. Toronto: University of Toronto Press: 1980.

Riddell, Agnes R. *Flaubert and Maupassant: A Literary Relationship*. Chicago: University of Chicago Press, 1920.

Saintsbury, George. *A History of the French Novel*. New York: Russell & Russell, 1964.

Sartre, Jean-Paul. *Situations II*. Paris: Gallimard, 1948.

Schopenhauer, A. "The World as Will and Idea," *The Works of Schopenhauer*, trans. W. Durant. New York: Simon and Schuster, 1931.

Schor, Naomi. *Breaking the Chain: Women, Theory, and French Realist Fiction*. New York: Columbia Unversity Press, 1985.

Steegmuller, Francis. *Maupassant: A Lion in the Path*. London: MacMillan, 1972.

Sullivan, Edward D., *Maupassant the Novelist*. Princeton: Princeton University Press, 1954.

———. *Maupassant: The Short Stories*. London: Arnold, 1962.

————. "Maupassant and the Motif of the Mask." *Symposium* 10 (1956): 34–41.

Targe, A., "Trois apparitions du Horla", *Poetique* 24 (1975): 446–59.

Thomas, H., and D.L. Thomas, *Living Biographies of Great Painters*. New York: Blue Ribbon Books, 1940.

Tolstoy, Leo. *Zola, Dumas, Guy de Maupassant*. Trans. E. Halperine-Kaminsky. Paris: Leon Chailly, 1896.

Trilling, Lionel. *Prefaces to the Experience of Literature*. New York: Harcourt Brace Jovanovich, 1979.

Wallace, Albert H. *Maupassant*. New York: Twayne Publishers, 1973.

West, T.G., "Schopenhauer, Huysmans and French Naturalism," *Journal of European Studies* 1 (1971): 313–24.

ACKNOWLEDGMENTS

How to Read and Why by Harold Bloom (New York: Scribner, 2000): pp. 42–46. © 2000 by Harold Bloom. Reprinted by permission.

The Modern Short Story: A Critical Survey by H.E. Bates (Boston: The Writer, Inc., 1941): pp. 73–74, 91–93. © 1941 by The Writer, Inc. Reprinted by permission.

"Shopenhauer, Flaubert, Maupassant: Conceptual Thought and Artistic 'Truth'" by G. Hainsworth from *Currents of Thought in French Literature* (Oxford: Basil Blackwell, 1965): pp. 183–184, 184–185. © 1965 by Basil Blackwell. Reprinted by permission.

Style and Vision in Maupassant's Nouvelles by Matthew MacNamara (New York: Peter Lang, 1986): pp. 1–4, 7. © 1986 by Peter Lang Publishing. Reprinted by permission.

Maupassant in the Hall of Mirrors by Trevor A. Le V. Harris (London: The Macmillan Press Ltd., 1990): pp. 38–41. © 1990 by The Macmillan Press Ltd. Reprinted by permission.

Gustave Flaubert: Letters by Gustave Flaubert, Trans. J.M. Cohen (London: Weidenfeld and Nicolson, 1950): pp. 231–232. © 1950 by Orion Books. Reprinted by permission.

"The Romanticism of Guy de Maupassant" by Olin H. Moore from *PMLA* 33, no. 1 (1918): pp. 101, 103–104, 113–114. © 1918 by the Modern Language Association of America. Reprinted by permission of the Modern Language Associate of America.

The Art of French Fiction by Martin Turnell (London: Hamish Hamilton; New York: New Directions, 1959): pp. 206–208. © 1959 by Martin Turnell. Reprinted by permission of New Directions Publishing Corp.

Literary Reviews and Criticisms by Prosser Hall Frye (New York: Gordian Press, 1968): pp. 197–198; 200–202. © 1968 by The Gordian Press. Reprinted by permission.

"Guy de Maupassant" by Joseph Conrad (London: Thomas J. Wise, 1919): pp 1–2. © 191 by Joseph Conrad. Reprinted by permission.

Demons of the Night: Tales of the Fantastic, Madness, and the Supernatural from Nineteenth-Century France by Joan C. Kessler (Chicago: University of Chicago Press, 1995): pp. xlii–xliii, xliv–xlv: © 1995 by The University of Chicago. Reprinted by permission.

Possible Worlds of the Fantastic: The Rise of the Paranormal in Fiction by Nancy H. Traill (Toronto: University of Toronto Press, 1996): pp. 129–132. © 1996 by Nancy H. Trail. Reprinted by permission.

Studies in Europeon Literature by Janko Lavrin (London: Constable & Company, 1929): pp. 183–184, 186–187. © 1929 by Constable & Company. Reprinted by permission.

"The Supernaturalism of Maupassant" by Ernest George Atkin from *PMLA* 42, no. 1 (1927): pp. 205–207. © 1927 by the Modern Language Association of America. Reprinted by permission of the Modern Language Association of America.

INDEX OF
Themes and Ideas

Monsieur Phillippe in, 43, 53; Monsieur Pimpesse in, 53; plot summary of, 38–41; Monsieur Poulin in, 38, 43, 53; Raphaele in, 38, 42, 52; the relationship between the ladies and their clientele, 51–56; Constance Rivet in, 39–40, 42, 44, 54; Joseph Rivet in, 38–40, 42–44; Madame Rivet in, 39–40, 43; Rosa in, 38–40, 42–43, 53–55; Madame Tellier in, 12–13, 38–46, 51–54, 56; Monsieur Tournevau in, 38, 41, 43, 53; Monsieur Vasse in, 53, 56